Praise for Jackson Hole Settlement Chronicles

A fascinating account of the first inhabitants of Jackson Hole: illegal squatters, rustlers, game poachers, and other outlaws rubbing up against legitimate homesteaders and ranchers. True tales of shootouts, Indian fights, and vigilante confrontations share the pages with respectable men who quietly built cabins, guided sport hunters, dug irrigation ditches, gardened, and peacefully made the Tetons their home. Oh, and once you've read the author's book, you'll no doubt want to wear a red bandana while in Jackson Hole. – Jim Hardee, editor, *Rocky Mountain Fur Trade Journal*, and author of *Pierre's Hole: The Fur Trade History of Teton Valley, Idaho*, Tetonia, Idaho.

A new and different perspective on Jackson Hole's earliest settlers: living in total isolation and braving brutal winters, they relied on wild game and predator bounties for subsistence and livelihood. Based on extensive research and richly illustrated with historic photographs, the author details the lives of the first settlers and Jackson Hole's infamous frontier rabble. A must read for anyone who loves Wyoming and Jackson Hole. – Robert C. Rudd, artist and local historian, author of *They Settled Here: Homesteads and Cabins of Jackson Hole*, Victor, Idaho.

I've read many accounts of early Jackson Hole, but this one presents the history from mostly a new and different point of view. The author leads us through the man versus nature hardships in the settlement of this remote country, but conversely, he also shows us how the early settlers depended on and benefited from nature, and how that evolved into some local citizens recognizing a need for game laws and conservation. The author gives us a taste of whom the early rugged, non-conforming pioneers were, how they lived, where they lived, and perhaps why they came to Jackson Hole, from those that stayed in the valley only a few years to those whose descendents still leave their footprints on the ongoing history. It's a story about the valley put in a context we haven't previously seen, with episodes that I had not heard of before. – Harold Turner, outfitter, guide, Triangle X Guest Ranch partner, life-long resident Jackson Hole.

The author melds human and natural history into a dramatic tale of how wildlife abundance has attracted people to Jackson Hole and sustained them from the earliest human inhabitants up through contemporary time; and how the conservation of its iconic species continues to set Jackson Hole apart from much of the modern world. While the glorious mountains made Jackson Hole a Mecca for travelers, its wildlife actually gave the valley its uncommon power of place. This is a book that speaks to the values of Nature; it will leave you inspired. – Todd Wilkinson, editor, the on-line *Wildlife Art Journal*, national environmental journalist and columnist, biographer of media mogul and bison baron Ted Turner, Bozeman, Montana.

Earle F. Layser (signature)

THE JACKSON HOLE
SETTLEMENT
CHRONICLES

The Lives and Times of the First Settlers

Courtesy of Jackson Hole Historical Society and Museum 191.40461

Earle F. Layser

This book is dedicated to Pattie, my best friend,
loving wife, and unequaled companion on life's myriad trails.
We roamed the West, Jackson Hole and Yellowstone,
a Pennsylvania niche called Pine Creek, and explored far-off quarters, too;
sharing a grand passion for life, each other, and far-flung travel;
my enduring gratitude to Pattie, to all her brightness and joyful being.

CONTENTS

Acknowledgements   9

The Valley Poem   15

Preface   17

Jackson Hole Prior to Euro-American Settlement   **29**

   Chapter 1. The Original Inhabitants   29

   Chapter 2. The Mountain Men   37

   Chapter 3. Prospectors and Miners   43

   Chapter 4. Government Sponsored Exploration   49

      William F. Raynolds' 1860 Expedition   49

      William A. Jones' 1873 Expedition   51

      Lt. Gustaves Doane's 1876 Winter Expedition   51

      Ferdinand V. Hayden Expeditions   55

   Chapter 5. Progression Toward Euro-American Settlement   59

Euro-American Settlement   **67**

   Chapter 6. President Arthur Tours Jackson Hole   67

   Chapter 7. The Recognized First Permanent Settlers   71

      John "Johnny" Carnes and Millie Sorelle   77

      John H. Holland   80

   Chapter 8. Outlaws, Renegades or Ligitimate Settlers?   83

   Chapter 9. A Settlement Proudly Lacking in Decorum   93

   Chapter 10. A Sampling of Early Settler Biographies   107

      Moses V. Giltner   109

William F. Manning   111

Robert E. Miller   113

Frank L. Petersen   116

Chapter 11. The Cunningham Ranch Incident   121

Chapter 12. The Indian War of 1895   125

Chapter 13. Other Mountain Law Episodes   145

The Elk Tusk Poachers   145

The Sheep Wars   152

Chapter 14. Developed Homesteads Become a Commodity   157

Chapter 15. Moving On – Settling Isn't Necessarily Permanent   163

The Carnes Move to Fort Hall   163

John Holland Proves Up and Sells his Homestaed   165

The Hollands Move to Teton Basin   152

Chapter 16. Oregon Beckons – John and Maud   167
Move On Once More

Epilogue   177

Homesteading Terminology   183

Notes   189

Bibliography   221

About the Author   233

Praise for other Titles by Earle F. Layser   234

Hayden Expedition photographer, William H. Jackson, was the first to photograph the Tetons in 1872. His photographs of the Yellowstone-Teton region were instrumental in persuading Congress to establish Yellowstone National Park.

ACKNOWLEDGEMENTS

For the published research and accounts of others that I relied upon, I owe a great deal of debt. Without the work of many others this narration would not be possible. The citations in the Notes and the Bibliography crediting the numerous sources utilized to produce this book are testimony to that statement.

Those historians and authors included the keepers of Jackson Hole's many layers of lore and history, in particular: Marion Allen, Robert Betts, Lorraine Bonney, Edna Bradford, Frank Calkins, John Daugherty, Ken and Lenore Diem, Bonnie Kreps, Fern Nelson, Doris Platts, Robert Rudd, Bruce Smith, and Jermy Wight. There is risk in listing folks, I've no doubt inadvertently failed to mention important others; my sincerest apologies for any such failings.

For the generous assistance, and boundless patience of the organizations and individuals, who contributed their personal time, knowledge, and help, I extend my sincere appreciation. A random roll call of these folks includes:

William Chaney, volunteer historian for the National Elk Refuge, generously gave of his time and knowledge in searching for records relating to the homesteads and property transfers occurring on the refuge.

Ron Berger of Troy, Idaho, contributed an unpublished biography of Teton Basin pioneer James Berger, which provided the leads for information on John Holland's Horseshoe Creek Ranch in Teton Valley.

Lorraine Bonney kindly provided a copy of John Carnes obituary from her personal files in Kelly, Wyoming, and a transcript of the unpublished 1957, University of Wyoming, Enoch "Cal" Carrington interview.

Rena Croft of Lovell, Wyoming, provided invaluable and detailed biographical information for her grandfather Frank Petersen, including published material and previously unpublished family lore and photographs.

Doris Platts of Wilson, Wyoming, deserves extra recognition for her detailed research and publications on Jackson Hole history including the Cunningham Ranch incident and the life histories of John Cherry and Robert Miller, as well as her recording of other local history and lore before it was lost to time.

Lenore Diem arranged for the use the photograph of Binkley and Purdy from the Ken and Lenore Diem Collection at the American Heritage Center in Laramie.

For colleagues and friends who went the extra mile in reviewing all or portions of the manuscript and freely provided their knowledge, invaluable comments, and technical and editorial suggestions, I am both grateful and indebted. These folks included: James Hardee, Editor of the Fur Trade Journal; Robert Rudd, local historian, artist, and original Director of the Jackson Hole Historical Society and Museum; Harold Turner, lifetime Jackson Hole resident, Teton Wilderness guide and outfitter, and Triangle-X Guest Ranch partner (Harold also magically produced a copy of the Hedrick memoir from his ranch file drawer); and Todd Wilkinson, environmental journalist, columnist, and author.

Jeanne Anderson's contract writing services, Driggs, Idaho, applied a keen editorial eye and exhaustive final grammatical scrubbing to the manuscript. Where others feared to go, Jeanne splashed red ink. The result, I believe, is an improved read.

I relied upon a number of institutions and archives for their invaluable assistance. At the Jackson Hole Historical Society and Museum, Mindy Barnett and Shannon Williams were particularly helpful; at the American Heritage Center in Laramie, Hailey Woodall, and, in particular, John Waggener, provided exceptional assistance and went the extra mile in locating rare photographs; Linda Merigliano, U.S. Forest Service, for providing Robert Miller's portrait; and the Montana State Historical Society and Idaho State Historical Society photo archives.

John Burton and Kim Kuhn, reference librarians at Oregon's Albany County Public Library, accomplished what no other archivists had been able to do – they located John and Maud Holland's obituaries, found information on the Scio Hotel, and provided a newspaper account of the hotel fire taken from Carol Bates' self-published c1989 book, *Scio in the Forks of the Santiam*.

National, state, and county archives, and the Bureau of Land Management-General Land Office website, provided access to data bases, homestead case files, real-estate documents, photographs, and other pertinent records.

To all those institutions, historians, archivists, and individuals, who assisted this endeavor, my sincere gratitude. This book simply wouldn't have been possible without access to those records and the helpful assistance.

Additional thanks are owed Robert Rudd, who generously allowed permission to include his poem, *The Valley*. When I first read his nostalgic poem, after my book was in draft manuscript form, I was amazed how much our musings had independently traveled down similar wagon ruts. He, however, had traveled those paths more than forty years earlier.

Rudd also generously allowed permission to use the Charlie Shinkle Cabin sketch from his artist folio, *They Settled Here: Homesteads and Cabins of Jackson Hole* (1970). His sketch of the log structure heads each chapter. Rudd noted, "Shinkle once owned a 160-acre homestead, but lost it in a poker game. Charlie had palsy and people called him 'Shaky Shinkle.'"

The Shinkle cabin has been gone for years now. After Charlie died it was torn down. Rudd's sketch is a fine rendition of how a typical Jackson Hole bachelor settler's residence appeared in the early twentieth century, complete with unstacked firewood and implements hanging conveniently on the outside wall of the rough-built cabin.

The cover jacket was designed by graphic artist Miga Rossetti of Rossetti Designs, Wilson, Wyoming, using an original Stephen N. Leek early-twentieth century photograph. The black border is an historic artifact on the antique photograph. Leek was an early settler and advocate for Jackson Hole's elk who took up photography in order to promote the need to establish the National Elk Refuge. The photograph was provided courtesy of the Stephen N. Leek Collection, American Heritage Center, University of Wyoming, Laramie. Right from the first, Miga assumed a strong personal and professional interest in the job of designing and laying out an attractive and appealing book. Her work comes highly recommended by me.

Many deserved thanks are gratefully given to my wife, Pattie – artist, author, and helpmate – who put up with my hours at the computer and patiently listened to what must have seemed like endless amounts of historical esoterica. Pattie's smiling enthusiasm spilled over into ideas for presentation, design, and editing. Words of thanks and praise fall far short in expressing my true indebtedness to her, not only for this endeavor but others, too, and in all manner and kind of invaluable assistance. She has been a true hand-in-hand partner along life's myriad happy and sometimes challenging paths.

Finally, this history is based upon the interpretations, judgments, and research of the author, as well as his attempted artful and selective weaving together of widely varying source materials. Any resulting omissions, inaccuracies, mistakes or failures in its presentation are solely the responsibility of the author.

Earle F. Layser
Alta, Wyoming

The Charlie "Shakey" Shinkle cabin.
(Courtesy Robert Rudd)

THE VALLEY

They came looking for something
Young men anxious to build, nameless men running
Others wanting to start again.
Here was opportunity, hardship, isolation, obstacles.
Neighbors fifty miles and company of a dog.
Water – haul it, dig for it, dream about it.
Rocks and weeds, and oceans of sage.
Food – pack it, shoot it, grow it.
Gold? not enough to make one rich.
Work for the next guy, work for yourself.
Split wood – snow so high you can't see over.
Mountains, always the mountains.
Got to get around – out to the south – a barrier
The flatlander can't see over
But the Indian came and went with the snow
And called them sacred.
Wild creatures – all kinds of neighbors.
Open country – ragged, wild, beautiful.
Seasons, change; wind, hot, cold
Real experience.
You can't have it second hand.
So they came. Tried to change things if they could
Tried to understand things as they were.
Came and went.
Put down roots, stayed
 Lived, were born and died here.

– Robert C. Rudd, 1970

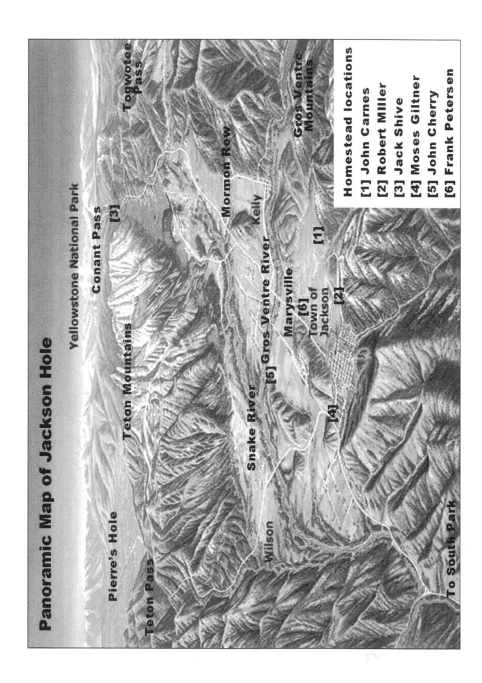

Panoramic Map of Jackson Hole

Yellowstone National Park
Togwotee Pass
Conant Pass [3]
Teton Mountains
Pierre's Hole
Teton Pass
Snake River
Wilson
Mormon Row
Kelly
Gros Ventre Mountains
[5] Gros Ventre River
Marysville [6]
Town of Jackson [2]
[1]
[4]
To South Park

Homestead locations
[1] John Carnes
[2] Robert Miller
[3] Jack Shive
[4] Moses Giltner
[5] John Cherry
[6] Frank Petersen

PREFACE

Unto a land flowing with milk and honey…
– Exodus 33:3

Jackson Hole is a name that ignites the imagination with images of the Old West, rugged snow-capped mountains, and a plentitude of wildlife. It is one of the most dramatic and compelling of North America's Rocky Mountain landscapes. The twelve by sixty mile valley is besieged on all sides by rugged mountains with lofty peaks and spires, while one of the Northwest's major waterways, the Snake River, surges from pristine Yellowstone headwaters, bisecting the entire length of the valley.[1] The sublime Teton Mountains and its iconic herds of elk are powerfully symbolic of Jackson Hole.

Our nation was built out of wildlands on the carcasses of the wild herds, the hides of fur bearers, and on the homelands of Native Americans. That statement rings particularly true for the settlement of Jackson Hole. The original settlers did not enjoy Arcadian lives of pastoral simplicity and idyllic joy. They struggled to fashion an existence out of profoundly isolated, and dramatically wild and rugged country, relying strictly on the natural resources at hand. Wildlife was a natural resource that played a singularly important role in Jackson Hole's settlement.

There has been no shortage of histories written about Jackson Hole. Some might ask, "Why write another?" Well, interestingly, while regional and local histories may make mention of the same personages and events, often the presentation and interpretation of the "facts" differ; the "gospel truth" exists in multiple variants. And different histories concentrate on different facets. This account presents new perspective and information on the very first settlers, their lives and frontier ethos, the incidents involving them, and especially, in recognizing the paramount importance of wildlife to the Hole's settlers and settlement. Today, residents and visitors alike, still continue to enjoy and be attracted to the valley for its wildlife and wildlands.

Histories written by people who were long-time residents, which are based on oral or folk tradition, handed-down tales and memories, and family alliances, sometimes, not too surprisingly, assume an underlying loyalty and defensiveness. They often tend to be more glowing in tone and perhaps unquestioning, too. Histories constructed from outside sources, official reports, archives, and more mundane but objective material and interpretations, can sometimes result in the same events being viewed quite differently. The latter, including this history, are less apt to accept or take for granted explanations of events and accuracy of the tales passed along from relatives and neighbors.

Some examples where recent research has led authors to different interpretations compared to traditional local histories may be found in: Edna Bradford's (2003) treatment of outlaw Teton Jackson, Kenneth and Lenore Diem's (1998) material on the Jackson Hole game poachers and elk tuskers, Jim Hardee's (2010) history of the fur trade in Pierre's Hole, and Jermy Wight's (2007) detailed research and analyses of Jackson Hole's 1895 Indian War.

Regardless, for Jackson Hole plenty of provocative material exists offering an opportunity to navigate between different methods and material to produce interesting, informative, and entertaining reading. Oral tradition, lore, and tales from long-time residents can be entertaining, true to the particulars as handed down, and in some cases, might even be said to be more compassionate and humane, while historical "facts" may sometimes portray or suggest another side to the story.

Jackson Hole's earliest Euro-American settlers, in the late-nineteenth century, were squatters; "settlers" may be much too generous a title. They lived under isolated, harsh, and primitive conditions, and by their own unwritten code and set of rules, including "Mountain Law." The Hole's settlement story is not about frills and lace in frontier log cabins, nor sunbonnets and covered wagons, rather it involves so called "bachelor settlers" and their struggle to put together a living on the borders of civilization. They were a rough and unruly bunch, but admirably enterprising, independent and self-sufficient, and frequently a bit eccentric. They relied heavily, and at times, totally, on exploiting the valley's abundant wildlife for subsistence and livelihood.

Many histories for the area begin only after the white man's arrival and activities. In reality, however, the valley was seasonally inhabited by Native Americans for thousands of years prior to its discovery and eventual colonization by Euro-Americans.

The first Euro-Americans to enter the mountain valley were trappers and fur traders; mountain men, mountaineers, or hunters as they were also called. They wandered into the legendary valley in the early nineteenth century trapping beaver and searching for trade routes. But European acculturation did not begin to follow until about eighty years later, near the close of that century.

While the industrial and urban age burgeoned elsewhere, Jackson Hole remained wild and remote, deeply isolated and apart from the explosive expansion of European civilization and industrialization elsewhere, protected by enormous distances and inaccessibility. Whatever was it that motivated individuals to settle in this uncivilized, off-the-map, inhospitable place? Certainly, as we will show, it was not easy living nor polite society.

Over the course of its history, the valley was host to a progression of romanticized western frontier figures: mountain men, fur traders, miners, explorers, outlaws, U.S. Army Cavalry, squatters, and bachelor settlers. However, if settlement is defined by the development of organized society – homesteading, farming, commerce, government, and law – then much of the earliest Anglo-American inhabitancy of Jackson Hole requires a benevolent interpretation of history to qualify.

The earliest settlers were so-called "bachelor settlers," or as they were apt to describe themselves, "bachelor trappers." That is not to say they all remained unmarried, over time many of them found wives and raised families in Jackson Hole. However, for an interval of time, bachelors predominantly comprised the citizenry of frontier Jackson Hole. Although they called themselves "trappers," and certainly did trap, these frontiersmen should not to be confused with the trappers or mountain men of the early part of the nineteenth century. Though there is little doubt that the Hole's bachelor trappers admired and tried to emulate the earlier mountain men.

The essentials of civilization were, if not disdained, at least mostly ignored by these early inhabitants of the valley. They viewed themselves not as settlers, homesteaders, or town builders, but rather as apart from society. As one person described them, they resembled "lone wolves … most of them lived like wild animals." Trapping, hunting, and guiding sport hunters – exploiting the region's wildlife for bounties, subsistence, hides, furs, trophy heads, and elk tusks – provided a living, generally not farming or ranching. As one of them stated in a memoir, they were a: "homeless, reckless, straight-shooting, and hard drinking set."[2]

These early arrivals in the valley were a mixed bag of frontiersmen and Old West characters: Civil War veterans, discharged soldiers, old

Indian fighters, Union Pacific Railroad construction workers, bull-whackers and freighters, prospectors and trappers, commercial hide and meat hunters, recent immigrants, runaways, down-on-their-luck miners, opportunists and refuges from the law. Dr. John Mitchell, a sport hunter visiting the Hole in1896, termed them: "a community of scalawags, renegades, discharged soldiers and predestined stinkers."[3] As civilization and industrialization relentlessly advanced elsewhere and the Old West dwindled, for a lingering interval in time, the denizens of Jackson Hole clung to and celebrated the western frontier's last hurrah.

The mountain men and fur traders left journals, accounts and letters; government expeditions filed extensive and detailed reports; but, for the most part, Jackson Hole's early bachelor settlers recorded little. The early history for Jackson Hole's settlement is generally sketchy, often contradictory, and frequently self-servingly embellished. One reason for this was that the early populace consisted largely of itinerant rabble: adventurers, drifters, fugitives, recluses and assorted frontier riff-raff who chose to pass their lives on the fringes of civilization; eccentric and colorful characters who preferred life outside of settlements and to be left alone. As times changed, some of those same personages reformed to become the Hole's leading and most up-standing citizenry.

The valley appealed to shadowy figures because it was a deeply remote and out-of-the-way place. Even after territorial law was established, the nearest law officer was located at Evanston, Wyoming, two-hundred and fifty miles by horseback. When winter's snow closed off the rugged mountain passes, no one could get in or out of the valley. The Hole was renowned to exist without benefit of the basic niceties of society, the law, or psychiatry – the ideal place for those wanting to escape from the rules of society, the tedium of honest employment, the encroachment of civilization, and any pressing need to reform or conform. The Hole's early squatters pretty much enforced their own code of law through "citizen committees," a polite way of saying justice by vigilante action or Mountain Law.

For an interval in time, the inhabitants of Jackson Hole were able to avoid close public scrutiny, shying away from having their lifestyles revealed or their history recorded. For benefit of outsiders, they made it a point to outrageously embellish, purposely obfuscate, or be reticent on what they were truly about – being able to do whatever they pleased without interference of any kind. They certainly did not fit the image of Hollywood's mythical and romanticized God-fearing, noble pioneers.

Violence and lawlessness prevailed in several early-day ruckus incidents involving vigilante actions. Examples are the 1892 Cunningham Ranch shootout, Jackson Hole's Indian War of 1895, and a nighttime warning delivered by masked riders to elk tuskers to clear out of the valley or be shot.

No historian has ever been able to satisfactorily reconstruct the 1892 Cunningham Ranch shootout where two cowboys – alleged horse rustlers – were gunned down by a posse recruited from the Hole's settlers. Afterward, the participants and Jackson Hole citizenry formed a protective "brotherhood." Details of the event were purposefully confounded by the participants and local residents to avoid possible retribution from both the law and outlaws. Today, the episode's "facts" exist in numerous variants, and locals are still apt to disagree about the event's details.

The Indian War of 1895 brought the settlers' attitudes and their Old West ethos into the National spotlight, as did the long fight to stop the illegal killing of elk for their teeth or tusks.

The 1895 Jackson Hole Indian War was about Native American federal treaty rights versus state's rights. Sparked by their racial animosity and aggressive self-serving actions, the settlers, supported by state officials, challenged federal authority to enforce Indian hunting and treaty rights.[4] Besides maliciously spreading rumors and bombastic falsehoods, the so called War involved the killing by settlers – some labeled it murder – of an old and near blind Bannock tribesman, wounding another and the capture of an Indian child. The politically calculated strategy to violently dispossess Native Americans of their treaty rights made the posse – comprised of twenty-seven original Jackson Hole settlers and the colluding State of Wyoming officials, appear anything but benevolent or law-abiding.

John H. Holland and John "Johnny" Carnes and his part Native American wife Millie Sorelle are traditionally credited with being Jackson Hole's "first permanent settlers" in 1884. But that recognition is not as clean and straight forward as most historians might have you believe. Complicating the claim is the fact other Euro-Americans were residing year-round in the valley in that same time period. For example, Army Lieutenant Gustaves Doane found John Pierce living in a crude cabin in Jackson Hole in 1876. What historically has served to define a settler versus others living year-round in the Hole in the same time period or earlier remains fuzzy at best. All the early residents relied principally on hunting and trapping for livelihood, not just gardening, farming or ranching.

While Carnes' and Holland's settlement is given in most histories as 1884, based on the year they horse packed some disassembled crude farm machinery into the valley, the title "first settlers" and date is beset with conflicting intrigues. Both men had already spent time in Jackson Hole beginning around 1877, both had filed for territorial water rights by 1883, and Holland and Carnes, along with another early settler, Mike Detwiler, are credited by some sources as already having a hundred-head of cattle in the valley by 1883. This history profiles the lives of Carnes and Holland before and after their arrival in Jackson Hole, and follows them to their final resting places.

Another early occupant of the valley, William Arnn, testified to Federal Marshals that he and Holland spent the winter of 1885 in Jackson Hole among notorious outlaws. The leader of those outlaws, Teton Jackson, later fingered Carnes and Holland for providing them with supplies. When Carnes and Holland were questioned by a posse at their Jackson Hole cabins in the autumn of 1885, they said their reason for being there was "trappin.'" Significantly, they did not say farming, ranching, or homesteading. If they viewed themselves as "permanent settlers" or homesteaders it wasn't something they chose to declare at the time.

Further confounding their settlement history, Holland testified in his 1894 homestead pre-exemption proof that he did not arrive in Jackson Hole until 1886. He stated that his first act was to "build a house," but that he did not establish residence there until 1887. His testimony is contradicted by the above 1885 posse report, his 1883 territorial water right filing, and other records and published histories.

Why falsify dates? Were the points in time simply confused? More likely, Holland had his reasons for muddling the dates – to avoid any possible self-incrimination or association with some of the shenanigans that went on in the early years in Jackson Hole.

Neither Holland nor Carnes proved up on their Jackson Hole homesteads until after 1896, twelve years after their customarily given 1884 settlement date. Histories generally state that both sold their homesteads before 1900 and left Jackson Hole. Usually that has been the end of the story for them. This account provides more complete information on Jackson Hole's celebrated first settlers, including what became of them after they left the area. In addition, life history information is given for ten other early day settlers, four of those in detail.

Jackson Hole harbored a classless society that celebrated individualism and eccentricity long after the frontier was declared to no longer exist; truly, the Hole really was "the last of the Old West." The early settler's ethos was classically western frontier. In a land of seemingly unlimited natural resources, they practiced self-reliance, endured hardships, and capitalized on the free "God-given" natural resources at hand for subsistence and livelihood. Of course, ignoring laws and having some luck helped, too.

Promoted as the Old West yet today – a replica designed by local artist and historian Robert Rudd of the original historic sign on Teton Pass reads: "...Yonder is Jackson Hole, Last of the Old West" – modern day Jackson Hole is hardly a parody of the way it was a century or more ago. If settlement is defined simply as inhabiting or colonizing the land, the process continues in modern times. For many things in Jackson Hole, change is only an illusion and a matter of degree.

Contemporary parallels with early-day history linger today. The valley continues to attract seekers: wannabe mountain men, Hollywood cowboys, adventure seekers, opportunists seeking fortunes, sportsmen looking for trophies, Nature seekers, and an itinerant element that moves on seeking a new or warmer clime after a few years. Exploitation continues to be a way of life – early Euro-Americans exploited the wildlife, "free land," and natural resources; residents today still exploit the wildlife, real estate, and tourists. Individualism and State's Rights, incorporating attitudes such as those that resulted in the Indian War of 1895, are still much touted. And a lot of the visitation by people is still in the form of "seasonal encampment," just as it was before recorded history; albeit, the seasonal and temporary encampment today has expanded up to a whopping 30,000 people nightly.

The valley has always conveyed a strong sense of place and engendered awe among the people visiting or occupying it, from Native Americans, mountain men, explorers, and pioneers, up to and including today's residents and visitors, many of whom are wealthy. It is a place of sublime extremes and deservedly strong adjectives. For many, Jackson Hole is as much a state of mind – an attraction to the romance – as the reality of the specific geographic area and features, not unlike it was more than a hundred years ago.

The mountains and the valley remain timeless; the human inhabitants change. The valley's history is not just an abstraction. An awareness of those who came before us, combined with the knowledge of the natural history and landscape, helps us define our sense of and connection to place – this place we call Jackson Hole.

> … I love old Wyoming,
> And I'm leaving her to you…
> Enjoy …but treat her gently, friend,
> 'Cause we're all just passin' thru.'
>   – Excerpt from poem by Howard Ballew,
>   Jackson Hole, c 1900-1997

Sheepeater Indians in front of their wikiup shelter.
(W. Henry Jackson photo courtesy NPS, Yellowstone National Park On-Line Digital Slide File #14826)

JACKSON HOLE PRIOR
TO EURO-AMERICAN SETTLEMENT

1
THE ORIGINAL INHABITANTS

For Indian country, [the Snake Country] was thickly inhabited, and may have contained 36,000 [native] souls or nearly one person to every four miles square. – Alexander Ross, *The Fur Hunters of the Far West.*

The original human inhabitants of the place we today call Jackson Hole were Native Americans. The high-elevation valleys surrounding the Teton Mountain Range were their ancestral hunting and foraging grounds where they seasonally encamped. These people were hunter-gatherers, living off the bounty of the land.

Archeological evidence indicates the presence of Native Americans as far back as eleven thousand years ago.[1] Euro-Americans entered the area only about two-hundred years ago; barely registering on a time-scale in comparison to how long aboriginal people had occupied the land.

In prehistoric time, people of the Absaroka (Crow), Bannock, Blackfoot, Northern Arapaho, Shoshone, and others such as the Nez Perce and Ute tribes, seasonally visited the valleys surrounding the Tetons. The Teton region was a crossroads, a place where the territories of the Absaroka, Blackfoot, and Shoshone people converged. In recorded time, it is written the Shoshone were particularly fond of the area about the Tetons. Family groups, such as Chief Washakie's band, seasonally encamped and hunted, for example, in Teton Valley in the 1850s[2] – a place the Indians called "Broad Valley." [3] Washakie's people ranged along the western slope of the Tetons and Jackson Hole and were referred to by other Shoshone as the "Elk-Eaters;" those that hunted buffalo on the plains were called "Buffalo-Eaters; and the Mountain Shoshone, "Sheep-Eaters."

In Jackson Hole, one known and apparently frequently-used aboriginal village site was situated along the north-end of Jackson Lake. Before the existing Jackson Lake dam was completed by Euro-Americans in 1916 (an earlier 1907 log crib dam washed out), meadows existed at the head of the lake. Artifacts from many different periods have been discovered from this lake-side area when water levels were low or drawn down.

Other known aboriginal sites are located on the northeastern part of what is today the National Elk Refuge, near Black Tail Butte, and at the mouth of Game Creek, south of today's town of Jackson at South Park. [4] The circular placements of stones to anchor tipi shelters, called "tipi rings," have been found at the Blacktail Butte site and in the upper Gros Ventre River valley. These examples of known encampment locations are based on archaeological evidence; undoubtedly other sites exist, too.

Archaeological excavations show Native Americans hunted and subsisted on bison, elk, and bighorn sheep within Jackson Hole. Those wildlife species and the rich habitat and hunting grounds the valley provided are a common link between the different people and cultures that have occupied the area over time. Aboriginal people, mountain men, explorers, settlers, down through time to contemporary sportsmen, have all pursued the same game species for livelihood, subsistence and sport within the environs of Jackson Hole. In fact, settlers' resentment of competition from Native Americans for wild game was the primary cause of the Indian War of 1895. The importance and value of wildlife to the people inhabiting the valley is timeless.

Down through the ages hunters have pursued game at some of the same specific locations that have proven to be advantageous. For example, archaeological evidence has shown aboriginal hunters frequently killed bison and elk along a narrow gulch located at the northeastern end of what is today the National Elk Refuge, a site which funnels animals through a topographical gap.[5] It is a place where modern-day sportsmen still stalk bison and elk. No doubt Native Americans once hunted bighorn sheep on Miller Butte. Early settlers certainly did, too.[6]

The high peaks of the Teton Mountain Range were called "the hoary headed fathers" by the Shoshone; other Native Americans referred to them as "the three brothers," and also, *teewinot*, meaning "many pinnacles." The snowy crags of the Tetons held special significance in the Shoshone's belief system: the peaks provided access to the spirit world and the power to heal and induce visions or dreams. A circular enclosure made from slabs of granite placed on a ledge three hundred feet below the Grand Teton summit is believed to have been constructed for the purpose of Native American "vision quest." Places along Jackson Hole's Snake River are also still considered spiritual sites by some Native Americans today. The valley has always had the power to generate awe and a strong sense of place among those who have peopled it, regardless of culture and race.

The Sheep-Eaters, also known as the Mountain Shoshone or

Tukudika, an ancient mountain people, resided in sustainable population densities throughout the Yellowstone Cordillera for thousands of years prior to European man's arrival. It is thought some of them may have lived year-round within the area, not just seasonally. They were hunter-gatherers who specialized in hunting the area's abundant mountain sheep for subsistence.

Known for their artistry in constructing bows incorporating the horn of bighorn sheep, the Sheep-Eaters produced prized weapons powerful enough to drive an arrow clear through a bison. Artifacts testify to their aboriginal presence high amid the Teton Range, such as those discovered on Spearhead Peak at 10,131-feet elevation and along the shores of the high-mountain lakes. The Mountain Shoshone were Jackson Hole's original mountain climbers. Keeping to high-elevations and remote areas, they escaped European influence and remained deeply immersed in the land and their ancestral ways. They were as one writer described, "human beings of a different kind."

In the ethnocentric and racially contemptuous manner of the era, Europeans judged the Mountain Shoshone to be miserably poor and destitute of all conveniences. However, mountain man Osborne Russell encountering the Mountain Shoshone in 1835, in what today is Yellowstone National Park's Lamar Valley, described them as "neatly clothed in dressed deer and [bighorn] sheepskins and perfectly happy."[7]

Native Americans mined obsidian – volcanic glass – for the manufacture of tools, projectile points, and for trade, at hidden extrusions in the Teton Range and in today's Yellowstone National Park at a place known as Obsidian Cliff. Obsidian cobbles can also be readily found along the Snake River, as well as soapstone at Berry Creek, which was used to manufacture pipes, totems, and implements, and for trade.

In a blink of the eye on a time scale, native people living, subsisting, and moving freely about the Teton Region, as they had done for millennia, came to a close, when, through federal treaty agreements and threats of U.S. military action, they were forced to move to and live on reservations.

As a result of the 1868 Fort Bridger Treaty, the Western Shoshone and Bannock moved onto the Fort Hall Reservation in Idaho, and the Eastern Shoshone and Northern Arapaho tribes located on the Wind River Reservation in Wyoming. The Absaroka were placed on the Crow Reservation in Montana through the 1870 Fort Laramie Treaty.

The Mountain Shoshone's age-old ways in the region came to a close, too, when Yellowstone National Park Superintendent Colonel P.W. Norris — after Custer's defeat in 1876, and on the heels of the Nez Perce fleeing across the park in 1877, along with the Idaho Sheep-Eater War of 1879 — acted to forcibly remove all Native Americans from the park. Norris feared the presence of Indians would conflict with the development and use of Yellowstone Park. The last of the Mountain Shoshone were rounded-up, removed from the Yellowstone Plateau, and escorted to the Wind River Reservation around 1879.

Conflict between Europeans and Native Americans continued to erupt sporadically throughout the western United States up until as late as 1923. But after the fur trade era ended in about 1840, Euro-American exploration and settlement within the Jackson Hole area experienced no conflicts for more than fifty years. The one little known, yet well publicized at the time, exception was Jackson Hole's Indian conflict in 1895.

Generally, overlooked in histories of the last Indian clashes in the West, the conflict involved Jackson Hole's settlers, peaceful reservation Indians, and what might be termed a conspiracy or calculated strategy between the State of Wyoming and Jackson Hole's earliest Euro-American residents to dispossess Native Americans of the hunting rights granted to them by the 1868 Fort Bridger Treaty. Aggressive action by white settlers, political maneuvering and intentional spreading of false rumors of Indian attacks and atrocities in Jackson Hole fueled national headlines, including coverage in the *New York Times*. However, it was the settlers who were actually the aggressors, not the Indians; the settlers' actions reflected Old West scorn for Native Americans as human beings.

It was neither Jackson Hole's nor the State of Wyoming's proudest time in history. Sharply defining a final ending to the Native American's ancient way of life in-and-around the Tetons, it was the last time a party of Bannock, Shoshone, or any other Native Americans, attempted to encamp and hunt in Jackson Hole as their ancestors had traditionally done for millennia, in spite of the fact that the 1868 treaty had provided them with that right.

Recently discovered tintype that appears to be renowned mountain man and
guide Jim Bridger.
(Courtesy Robert Coronato, Rouges Gallery, Hulett, Wyoming)

2
THE TRAPPERS

Everybody understood one thing in the mountains – that he must keep his life by his own courage and valor, or at least by his own prudence.
– Trapper Joseph Meek

The mountain men's name for the Shoshone Indians was "Snakes" or the Snake Indians.   By the early-nineteenth century, the high-elevation valleys in the Snake Country were well-known to Euro-American and French-Canadian mountain men or trappers, as they were also called.[8]

Fueled by Europe's insatiable demand for beaver fur, the trappers penetrated unknown and uncharted territory. In their characteristic independent ways, they coined their own terms for the things and places they encountered. The word valley was much too elegant for them. Instead, they called the untamed, high-elevation Rocky Mountain valleys that were encircled by mountains: "Holes."

The mountain men frequently named such places after fellow trappers or recognizable landscape features – Pierre's Hole, Brown's Hole, Gardner's [Gardiner's] Hole, Grey's Hole, Jackson's Hole, Ross's Hole, Burnt Hole, the Big Hole, and so forth. Many of the area's landscape features bear names that were originally given to them by the mountain men and fur traders.

Not all their names stuck, however. The Tetons were variously recognized as the Mad River Mountains, Pilot Knobs, Triple Snow Peaks, Three Titans, Three Paps, and Les Trois Tetons during this period.

Some believe John Colter, a member of the epic Lewis and Clark Expedition, may have been the first Euro-American to visit the mountain valley with the majestic mountains south of Yellowstone.[9] This would have occurred sometime around 1807 or 1808. But other historians do not believe Colter's route through the Yellowstone region brought him that far south. The evidence is inconclusive.[10] Today, Colter Peak in Yellowstone National Park is named after him.

Trapper John Dougherty, traveling with a small party of mountain men, passed through the awesome mountain valley in 1810.[11] They were intending to meet up with Andrew Henry's hunters, who had wintered along what would afterward become known as the Henry's Fork of the Snake River. From Henry's winter camp, near St. Anthony, the peaks of the Tetons visibly beckoned on clear winter days.

Dougherty's party of trappers may have actually been the first Euro-Americans to enter the mountain valley that would become known as Jackson Hole. The large beaver populations they discovered in Jackson Hole and the surrounding environs gave the area a legendary reputation among the trappers.

When Henry's band of hunters disbanded in the spring of 1811, trappers John Hoback, Edward Robinson, and Jacob Reznor, traveled through Jackson Hole on an intended return East. The Hoback River in Jackson Hole takes its name from John Hoback.

By some quirk of chance, in the vast wilderness, Hoback and his companions encountered Wilson Price Hunt, who was leading the Astorian's Pacific Fur Company's party, looking for fur and an overland trade route. Hoback, Robinson and Reznor agreed to guide the Astorians, leading them back over the same path the trio had just come, traversing the remarkable valley with the spectacular mountain range lying deep within the Snake Country. Hunt's party referred to the imposing peaks as the Pilot Knobs.[12]

Hunt's practical name for the lofty mountains didn't last. French-Canadian (Iroquois) trappers viewing the same peaks from the west-side of the range called them *Les Trois Tetons*, the three breasts, paps, or teats. The French-Canadian trappers' more imaginative name stuck.

Although Colter and Dougherty later assisted in preparing maps for the region, at that time, Hunt would not yet have had the benefit of those maps. The Tetons were mostly uncharted country to Europeans – *terra incognito*. Four men from Hunt's company remained behind in the awesome mountain valley to trap. They, as well as possibly Hoback, Robinson, and Reznor, were likely the first Euro-Americans to trap in Jackson Hole.[13]

Pierre Tevanitagon was among the early French-Iroquios trappers who hunted along the west-slope of the Tetons in 1818. He returned sometime later with the Northwest Fur Company and became tragically immortalized in a bloody encounter with the Blackfeet Indians. Although he was not actually killed in Teton Valley, the mountain men named the high-mountain valley on the west-side of the Tetons after him: *Trou a Pierre*, Pierre's Hole. Mormon settlers later renamed it Teton Basin; today, it is known as Teton Valley.

Seven years after Pierre's fatal run-in with the Blackfeet, David

"Davy" Jackson, trapper and field captain for the Rocky Mountain
Fur Company, spent time in 1825 along the shore of a large lake in
the wildly-remote mountain valley. Davy later returned for fall hunts
in 1829 and 1830. Tradition says the valley and lake were named after
him by his partner, trapper and trader William Sublette – Jackson's
Hole and Jackson's Lake.[14] Historian Vivian Talbot wrote: "…a town,
lake, and valley among the Tetons that bears his name are monuments
sufficiently sublime and enduring for any man."[15] Talbot failed to
also mention the two mountain peaks named after him – one in the
Gros Ventre Mountains and the other in the Wind River Range, both
called: Jackson Peak.

At one point, however, nineteenth century cartographers attempted to
rename the remote lake bearing Jackson's name to Biddle Lake. At age
seventeen, Nicholas Biddle was the first editor of the Lewis and Clark
Journals. Published in 1814, it is known as the Biddle-Allen edition
of the Journals. Naming the lake Biddle, however, did not stick.[16]

Many luminaries of the fur trade era passed through Jackson Hole,
including, Jim Bridger, Joe Meek, Jim Beckwourth, Thomas "Broken
Hand" Fitzpatrick, Osborne Russell, Jedediah Smith, and William
Sublette. The 1829 and 1832 fur-trade rendezvous were held in
Pierre's Hole, a gathering in which traders, trappers and Indians
from various tribes throughout the region met to carouse, trade for
supplies, and sell their pelts.

Some of the trappers and native tribesmen en route to or from
the Pierre's Hole rendezvous traveled through Jackson Hole. The
mountain men discovered and followed the passes and trails in-and-
out of the valley, pathways that had been in use by Native Americans
from time immemorial.

Journals left to us by the fur traders and trappers refer to the

following: a "gap in the mountains south of the *Trois Tetons*" –
today's Teton Pass, highway 22 (the original route probably followed
Mosquito Creek, rather than today's location); an "ascent of the Gros
Ventre" River to the Green River basin – a trail route, which as we'll
see, played a significant role in Jackson Hole's settlement history; a
pathway leading down the Hoback River and into Jackson Hole –
today's highway 189; Togwotee Pass – highway 26; and others, such
as across the northern-end of the Teton Range into Jackson Hole or
Yellowstone – the Conant Trail (author Owen Wister's "Horse Thief
Trail") at Berry Creek.[17]

Fur company principal and trader, William Sublette, was the first
to bring wagons into the Rocky Mountain region. Pulled by mules
in 1830, Sublette proved to aspiring Euro-American settlers that
wheeled travel was a practicable way to reach the far regions of the
West.[18]

Historian Bernard DeVoto credits the crusty mountain men with
"intimately knowing every inch of the land and streams." In their
quest for fur, adventure, and new country, they ventured into the
most distant, uncharted, and remote places. While the mountain men
generally had a disdain for civilization, they nevertheless led the way
for the Euro-American exploration and settlement that followed.

Prospector and miner Karl "Uncle Jack" Davis is shown here with his packhorses loaded with a quartered elk. Born in 1827, Davis reportedly fled to Jackson Hole in the late-nineteenth century to escape the law after allegedly killing a man.

(Courtesy Jackson Hole Historical Society and Museum BC #0281)

3

PROSPECTORS AND MINERS

"Uncle Jack" Davis was a gold miner... a colorful character, he devoted himself to prospecting in the Snake River Canyon, where he had a crude cabin. When he died in 1911, his valuables consisted of $12 in cash and about the same amount in gold amalgam. Not much return for at least 20 years of prospecting. – John Daugherty, *A Place Called Jackson Hole*.

For a few decades after a decline in fur prices and fur trade, which happened around 1840, there is little record of white men visiting Jackson Hole. The valley returned to being seasonally peopled by Native Americans. Later, after the mid-nineteenth century, miners and government sponsored expeditions were the next Euro-Americans to enter the valley.

A four-letter mineral motivated the miners: gold. Prospecting was a chance to strike it rich, but the odds of that were similar to winning a modern day lottery.

When prospects ran out (or perhaps when they were at a high) within the boomtown mining camps in the geographic region, such as at Virginia City, Montana, and South Pass, Encampment, and Miners' Delight, Wyoming, the miners sometimes struck out in the safety of large parties to investigate and prospect new areas. The rush of prospectors and miners to explore a new area was dubbed a "stampede."

The early-day prospectors were generally an uncouth lot, but were similar to the trappers in one respect: they explored up all the drainage ways. Mountain men had looked for beaver along the streams and headwaters, the prospectors searched the same tributaries for gold. In truth, few discovered riches or became wealthy.

In 1862, a large group of prospectors and miners that had elected themselves to be led by Walter W. DeLacy, an engineer, entered Jackson Hole by way of the Snake River Canyon. DeLacy later spoke of this particular assemblage of miners as "the 40 thieves," which gives a clue to the esteem in which he regarded them.

DeLacy kept a journal, in which he described the real riches of Jackson Hole: "[It is] one of the most picturesque basins in the mountains … covered with fine grass; the soil is deep in many places and is capable of settlement." He prophesized, "it will [someday] in the future be covered with bands of cattle and sheep."[19]

Part of DeLacy's stampede continued on through what is today's southwest corner of Yellowstone Park. DeLacy Creek in Yellowstone is named after him. Afterward, DeLacy assisted in the preparation of the first map for that part of the park.[20]

DeLacy's party, as well as other miners that followed over the years, found "color" in the gravels throughout the Upper Snake and its tributaries. Encouraged, prospectors repeatedly scoured all the drainage ways in search of the "mother lode," the source of the fine gold flecks, without success.

Three decades later, in 1895, more than one hundred men were

Later in life portrait of engineer Walter DeLacy who led a large party of miners through Jackson Hole and the southwest corner of Yellowstone in 1863.
(Courtesy NPS, Yellowstone National Park On Line # 02952)

reported to be engaged in prospecting and placer mining in the
vicinity of Crystal Creek, a tributary of the Gros Ventre River.[21]
Relic remains of an abandoned "ball machine" from more recent
years, used for ore rock smashing and grinding, still exist along
Crystal Creek.

Other attempts at mining occurred in the Jackson Hole area at Berry
Creek, Cottonwood Creek on the Gros Ventre, Ditch Creek, and
in the Snake River Canyon. The first sawmill in Jackson Hole was
built by the Whetstone Mining Company around 1889. Located at
the junction of Pacific and Whetstone Creeks, at the northern-end
of Jackson Hole, the Whetstone mining operation lasted until 1897
before shutting down.[22]

Tales of gold-rich gravels in the Snake Country proved to be
unfounded. Delacy's party, and other prospectors, placer miners,
and mining companies that followed over the years, were not able
to find or retrieve sufficient quantities of the lustrous metal within
the Jackson Hole area to make their efforts worthwhile. Otherwise,
as historian John Daugherty has pointed out, the valley's landscape
would look much different today as a result of boomtowns,
timbering, stream bottom dredging and excavations, scarred hillsides,
and the other disruptive activities which generally followed in the
wake of gold discoveries. [23]

A grim reminder of the miner's early-day presence in Jackson Hole
remains today along the Snake River, north of the Snake River
Overlook above Moose. In 1886, at what has become known as
"Deadman's Bar," four prospectors from Montana set up a placer-
mining operation. Sometime afterward, a gruesome discovery was
made – the bodies of three of the men lying in the river weighted
down by rocks. A sheriff's posse tracked the fourth member of the
party to Teton Basin, where they arrested him. He was taken to

Evanston, Wyoming, the county seat for Jackson Hole in those years, and tried for murder, but claimed self defense. Since there were no witnesses, a frontier jury acquitted him.

Hayden exploration party members posing before their tents while in camp.
(Courtesy NPS, Yellowstone National Park, On Line #14826)

4
GOVERNMENT SPONSORED EXPLORATION

This side trip to the Tetons was really secondary to the main object of the expedition, but by this time Yellowstone had lost something of its novelty, and the Tetons never before photographed, now became of the first importance, so far as I was concerned.
– William H. Jackson, Hayden Survey photographer, 1872.

After the mid-nineteenth century, the United States Government began sponsoring expeditions to explore the valley and its surrounding environs – surveying, mapping, reporting findings, and verifying in the process, what had earlier been discounted as tall tales told by untrustworthy mountain men.

The published government surveys made the general populace more aware of Jackson Hole, its unclaimed lands, natural resources, and wild game populations. It attracted the general public's attention to what lay beyond in the far-flung Rocky Mountains, contributing information leading toward and encouraging western expansion and settlement.

William F. Raynolds' 1860 Expedition
Captain W.F. Raynolds' 1860 expedition was guided by renowned mountain man Jim Bridger. Dr. Ferdinand V. Hayden, who later

became the leader of notable 1872, 1877, and 1878 expeditions, was a member of the party.

Bridger guided the expedition on an old Indian trail to a place the Native Americans appropriately called "Land of Many Rivers." Raynolds recorded the spot as "Union Pass;" although the mountain men used it and knew about it, they had never named it. Located on the Continental Divide, this unique topographic feature is where the headwaters for three major western river systems unite – the Green/Colorado, Snake/Columbia, and the Wind/Missouri. The 11,675-foot elevation peak southeast of the pass is known as "Three Waters Mountain," a topographical marvel, a triple-divide peak.[24]

Terrain and snow forced Raynolds' party to seek a route through Jackson Hole, where the valley's meadows were described as "flower-painted." They became the first government survey to pass through and explore the valley. The Snake River was roiled with springtime runoff and it took three days to cross; one member of the party drowned in the process.

From Jackson Hole, Jim Bridger guided the expedition on the old Indian trail over Teton Pass into Pierre's Hole. After the expedition's difficult experience of traveling across the mountainous terrain, Raynolds concluded in his report that "the Jackson Hole and Yellowstone country were too mountainous for a railroad."[25]

Contrary to Raynolds' observations, fifty-three years later, in 1913, the Oregon Short Line was built from St. Anthony, Idaho, into and through Teton Valley to the town of Victor. Earlier, another spur had been constructed from Rexburg and St. Anthony to Ashton, Idaho, and from there to West Yellowstone, Montana. The railroad spurs were advertised as the: "Teton Mountain routes to Yellowstone National Park."

Raynolds' assessment proved partly true however, as the railroad never reached Jackson Hole; Victor, Idaho, was as close as it got.[26] For years, from the end of the line at Victor, visitors and commerce had to endure rugged and exhausting travel by wagon, buckboard, or horseback along the old Indian route across Teton Pass to reach Jackson Hole.[27]

William A. Jones' 1873 Expedition
In 1873, Captain W.A. Jones conducted a survey through the Yellowstone or Snake Country for the purposes of locating a military road. His party spent a month in the newly created National Park. During that time, all but one of his Shoshone guides rebelled, leaving the party stranded south of Yellowstone Lake in what is today the Teton Wilderness Area.

Traveling south, the group discovered and found their way eastward across a mountain pass. They named the pass after their lone Shoshone guide, Togwotee (meaning "spear thrower"). In his report, Jones recommended construction of a wagon road north from the Union Pacific railroad line across Togwotee and Two Ocean passes to access Yellowstone National Park.

Fortunately, the road was never built, leaving us instead, today, with the congressionally designated Teton Wilderness Area. When combined with the unroaded area in adjacent Yellowstone National Park, it represents one of the largest expanses of unroaded wildlands remaining in the conterminous United States. [28]

Lt. Gustaves Doane's 1876 Winter Expedition
In an epic 1876 winter trip, members of the Lt. Gustaves Doane expedition barely survived. Traveling south from Yellowstone, they entered Jackson Hole on November 23. They described their expedition as an "Arctic one."

Portrait of Lt. Gustaves Doane whose winter exploration of Jackson Hole in 1876 nearly met with disaster. (Courtesy NPS, Yellowstone National Park On Line # 02939)

Enroute from Yellowstone, they missed the easier Indian trail located along the east side of Jackson Lake. Instead, they made their way along the heavily-timbered, boulder-strewn west shore. For rations, they were forced to eat their horses. Lt. Doane commented that "horse flesh tasted exactly as the perspiration of the animal smells." Fishing was good, but Doane believed fresh fish was "too thin a diet to subsist on alone." The expedition turned into a challenge for survival.

Undaunted, however, Doane recorded that the moonlight view of the Teton Mountains in Jackson Hole was "one of unspeakable grandeur."

In Jackson Hole, they were surprised to discover John Pierce living in a crude cabin in what is now South Park. No doubt Pierce was just as surprised to see them, too. Pierce gave Doane and his men some elk meat.

The expedition attempted to leave Jackson Hole by boating down the Snake River through the canyon. It proved to be another disaster; they capsized in the icy turbulent rapids. Doane lost his journal in the river. They were lucky no one lost their life. Somehow they managed to make it to Fort Hall in January 1877.

Fort Hall was located on the Snake River near today's Pocatello, Idaho, on what is now the Fort Hall Indian Reservation. The Fort was established in 1834 by Natheniel Wyeth of the Hudson's Bay Company. Situated on the old Oregon Trail, it was the only Euro-American outpost in the Oregon Country at the time. Reached by following the Snake River – normally from Pierre's Hole to avoid the Snake River Canyon – the Fort was roughly 170 miles from Jackson Hole. In 1880, Baillie-Grohman reported that it could be "reached in seven or eight days by Indian trails."[29]

By the time Doane's party arrived at Fort Hall in mid-winter, Doane

Government exploration parties relied on game meat to supplement their provisions. In this W.H. Jackson photograph, Hayden party hunters have killed a half dozen bull elk for camp meat. (*Courtesy NPS, Yellowstone Park On Line #02931*)

had lost 64 pounds, from a vigorous 190 pounds down to a scrawny 126.[30] Doane Peak in the Tetons is named after him.

F.V. Hayden Expeditions

The most renowned and well-funded of the government surveys in the Yellowstone region were the expeditions conducted by Dr. Ferdinand V. Hayden and his party members in 1872, 1877, and 1878. Hayden, a geologist by training, had earlier been given the name "Man-Who-Picks-Up-Rocks-Running" by the Sioux Indians.[31]

The Hayden expeditions included exploration of the Yellowstone area, the Teton Mountain Range, Pierre's Hole, and Jackson Hole. The 1872 party had sixty-one men, including such notable personages as: botanist John M. Coulter, biologist C. Hart Merriam, topographer Gustavus Bechler, geologist Frank Bradley, geologist Orestes St. John, photographer William H. Jackson; and in a later expedition, artist Thomas Moran. Mountain man Richard "Beaver Dick" Leigh, who was residing in Pierre's Hole with his first family in those years, served as their guide.

Some of the contributions of the Hayden party members included: Nathaniel P. Langford and John Stevenson claimed to be the first Euro-Americans to successfully summit the Grand Teton;[32] artist Thomas Moran painted and sketched his renowned Yellowstone scenes; and William Jackson made the first photographs of Yellowstone and the Tetons, noted by Hayden to be "several magnificent views." Some of his photographed scenes of the Teton Mountains were from the summit of Table Mountain on the west-side of the mountains. Jackson had to horse pack and carry his heavy equipment up to the 11,106-feet Table Mountain summit.[33]

Hayden was a strong supporter of designating the Yellowstone area a national park and Moran's paintings, Jackson's photographs, and

Hayden party photographer W.H. Jackson with assistant setting up on the summit of Table Mountain at 11,106-feet elevation to capture his 1872 image of the Grand Teton. (Courtesy NPS, Yellowstone National Park On Line # 031230)

the expedition's reports were instrumental in persuading Congress to establish Yellowstone National Park in 1872, the Nation's first national park.

In Jackson Hole, Hayden party surveyors named the lakes along the eastern base of the Teton Range and other prominent features, many of those in honor of expedition members, including Mount Moran, Leigh Lake, Jenny Lake, Taggart Lake, Phelps Lake, Blacktail Butte, Mt. Leidy, and Mt. St. John. The beautiful waterway that today is named String Lake, they originally called Beaver Dick Lake. They re-titled the towering pinnacle known as the Grand Teton to Mount Hayden, after their expedition leader. But that nomination failed to displace the long-standing French-Canadian trapper's name for the range's highest peak. Hayden Valley in Yellowstone National Park, however, bears the expedition leader's name.[34]

Historians identify the Hayden Surveys as the most significant of the region's exploration expeditions. The 1878 survey is considered by historians to have marked the last of the age of exploration and discovery in the West.[35]

Mountain man Richard "Beaver Dick" Leigh with Jenny and his first family. Leigh was the first Euro-American to make Pierre's Hole his permanent home. Leigh served as a guide for the 1872 Hayden Expedition. (Courtesy Jackson Hole Historical Society and Museum 1958.2342.00)

5

PROGRESSION TOWARD EURO-AMERICAN SETTLEMENT

I heard from a trapper, Dutch George, the only human being, so far as I could learn that had ever wintered [in Jackson Hole]...he told me that for three months the roof of his cabin was flush with the white pall... when the snow finally melted, the creeks and rivers were so high he was imprisoned till the end of July...he had not seen a single other human being for ten months. – William Baille-Gorhman, 1880.

Jackson Hole has always been known for its remoteness, hard winters, wildlife, and spectacular setting. It was a singular outpost where extreme weather, a short-growing season, and deep isolation defied traditional Euro-American settlement. More than twenty years after the Homestead Act of 1862, over fifteen years after the first Wyoming territorial government assembly met in 1869, and more than a decade after Yellowstone National Park was established in 1872, the valley still boasted no permanent settlers.

In those bygone times, snow sealed off the mountain passes preventing anyone from getting in or out of the valley in winter. And when spring snowmelt swelled the mountain streams and rivers, it likewise shut off travel. The secluded valley offered a snow-bound hideaway for scoundrels wanting to evade the law. In his 1876 winter reconnaissance, Lt. Doane had recorded: "Jackson's Hole was a favorite rendezvous for desperadoes and thieves."

The first Euro-American to take up lifelong residence within the area surrounding the Tetons was mountain man Richard "Beaver Dick" Leigh. Author Edna Bradford credits Leigh as being the "the first settler" within the Teton region.[36] Leigh's nick name referred to his beaver trapping skills. In an undated diary entry, he penned: "...i ave followed my profeson as trapper hunter and guide in that section of cuntry [the Tetons]...since 1863."[37]

Leigh was born in 1831 in Lancashire, England. He ran away at age sixteen, a stowaway on a ship headed to America; he joined the Hudson's Bay Company; and later, fought in the Mexican War.[38] Along with his Shoshone wife, Jenny, and family (and later, his second wife, Tadpole, who he married when she was fourteen years of age), Dick Leigh made Pierre's Hole his home from 1863 until his passing in 1899. Although they may have planted a garden at times, the Leighs did not farm or ranch in a traditional sense, but lived off the land, camping seasonally throughout the area.

Leigh also maintained a cabin at the meadows at the north-end of Jackson Lake, regularly using the old Indian trail across the northern part of the Teton Mountain Range to travel between Pierre's Hole and Jackson Hole. Known today as Conant Pass, it is a route and pass which Leigh named after Al Conant who reportedly came into the Tetons in 1865. [39]

In 1872, the Hayden Expedition employed Leigh as a guide. Expedition cartographers named several well-known local features after Leigh and his wife Jenny: Leigh Canyon, North and South Leigh Creeks, Leigh Lake, and the glittering gem at the mouth of rugged Cascade Canyon, Jenny Lake. Leigh, encouraged by Hayden Party members, kept a journal for the years 1873-1879. In one entry, he penned: "Teton Basin was the beautifulest sight in the whole world."[40]

Dick Leigh suffered a heart-breaking tragedy in 1876, when Jenny and all six of their children died of smallpox. Leigh remarried, this time a Bannock woman named Susan Tadpole, and they raised a family of three children.

In a chance encounter in 1892, while camped near Two Ocean Pass south of Yellowstone (possibly at the Snake River Meadows), Dick Leigh met Theodore Roosevelt, who, along with his small party, were hunting in what was then deep and uncharted wilderness. Roosevelt wrote of that encounter, that they "came upon mountain man Beaver Dick... living in a skin tepee with his comely wife and half breed children," remarking that Leigh "had quite a herd of horses, many of them mares and colts."[41]

Settled earlier and more rapidly, Pierre's Hole on the west-side of the Tetons, has always had a significant connection to Jackson Hole by virtue of Teton Pass and the Teton Mountain Range. Pierre's Hole, however, unlike the more rugged and topographically contained Jackson Hole, is more readily accessible. It opens out onto rolling, broad plains to the northwest. By virtue of its geography and greater accessibility, it is logical that Teton Valley would have attracted permanent Euro-American settlement before Jackson Hole. One of Leigh's last journal entries reads: "i ave the pleashur of knowing that i ave led the settlements on the snake river..."

In 1882, Hiram C. Lapham, his family, and brother arrived in Pierre's Hole. They practiced livestock ranching and are generally recognized as the first settlers on the west side of the Teton Mountains. Bachelor settlers Chris Sorenson, Robert Benbrook and Sam Hill built cabins in Teton Basin that year, too. By 1883, a half-dozen families had followed. The closest post office at that time for Pierre's Hole and Jackson Hole, too, was Rexburg, Idaho. Tim Hibbert, a Teton Valley resident of that era, would make the horseback trip to Rexburg and back for the mail in "one sunup-to-sundown ride," a distance of about seventy miles. [42]

Latter-Day Saints scouting Pierre's Hole for colonization around that time were warned that it was occupied by "horse thieves and outlaws;" nevertheless waves of Mormon settlers began pouring into Teton Basin by 1888.

During this early period, it's known too, that a scattering of Euro-Americans were also occasionally over-wintering in Jackson Hole, such as John Pierce, who Doane's party discovered living in a crude cabin at the south-end of Jackson Hole in the winter of 1876.

Historian Jermy Wight credits John Pierce as being Jackson Hole's "first permanent [Euro-American] resident in 1876."[43] Daugherty also credits a John Pierce with being among Jackson Hole's earliest pioneer settlers.[44] If it is the same John Pierce that both Dick Leigh and Lt. Doane mention in their journals from that year, it means Pierce was actually residing in the Hole at least ten years before the date generally attributed to him in the literature for being "among Jackson Hole's earliest settlers."[45]

Among the earliest settlers in Pierre's Hole, frontiersman David Breckenridge's life story was similar to others of the frontier era. Born in 1850, he left his Springfield, Illinois, home as a teenager believing he had killed his half brother after hitting him with an ox yoke during a fight. David found a job on a Mississippi steamboat, after which he drifted through Arkansas and into Texas. In Brownwood, Texas, he worked in a butcher shop and became the town's first marshal. Next he found his way to the gold camps in Colorado, and worked as a miner at the Cripple Creek strike in Leadville. Not discovering riches in the gold camps, he tried trapping at Gypsum Creek, Colorado.

Reportedly, he made more money trapping that winter than at any previous work.[46] Encouraged, David and a friend, Frank Summers, headed out for the Idaho and Wyoming Territories to make their fortunes trapping in the fur trade's fabled Pierre's Hole and Jackson's Hole.

Breckenridge and Summers arrived in Pierre's Hole in 1881 and struggled through the first winter holed up in the gorge of Canyon Creek west of present day Tetonia, Idaho. They made their way over Teton Pass to Jackson Hole in 1883-84, where they trapped with Jim Goodwin, the individual for whom Goodwin Lake in the Gros Ventre Mountains is named. Breckenridge later claimed he and his partners were the only Euro-Americans living in Jackson Hole that winter. [47]

In 1884, while Breckenridge was looking for a place to ford the Snake River in Jackson Hole to return to Teton Basin, Breckenridge's family tradition says he encountered early Jackson Hole settler Robert Miller, who was also searching for a ford, but from the other side of the river. Breckenridge moved back to the west side of the Tetons in 1884, where he purchased a relinquishment right from a squatter near today's town of Tetonia and took up homesteading.[48]

Undoubtedly, others also came and went anonymously and unrecorded in Jackson Hole in those early years, passing through and residing only briefly or seasonally. If asked their purpose for being there, it is certain they would have replied "trappin," the western frontiersman's amorphous and catchall occupation. Again, these men should not be confused with the trappers or mountain men of the fur trade era decades earlier. Rather they were part of a restless breed – frontiersmen, adventurers, outlaws, wanderers, and fortune hunters, searching out the borders, trying to avoid civilization even as it closed in around them. Mostly, they left little or no record of having passed through. Those with a shady past and an aversion for society preferred

Portrait of early-day trapper and Pierre's Hole settler David Breckenridge.
(Courtesy Teton Valley Museum, Driggs, Idaho)

it that way. As one writer noted, it was a "place to lose one's identity as well as one's pursuer." [49]

Some though, such as Breckenridge, eventually chose a different existence: they settled, homesteaded, and became life-long residents within the shadows of the Tetons, establishing family legacies through a connection to the land. [50]

Teton Pass and the Conant trail were primary ways to access Jackson Hole during this early era. The Native American trail on Teton Pass evolved into a rugged wagon road, linking the valley to settlements in Pierre's Hole, and eventually, in 1913, to the railhead at Victor, Idaho. The Conant trail was an important wagon road and livestock driveway in the early years for northern Jackson Hole, but it fell out of use after Jackson Lake dam was completed in 1916 and impounded water cut off part of the trail.

Teton Pass facilitated Jackson Hole's communication and development from the beginning, including the fur trade era and earliest settlement days; it still serves as a primary artery for commerce and transportation. Where Native Americans and trappers once trod, and pioneers followed, today's modern commuter traffic travels at alarming speeds.

United States President Chester A. Arthur (center) and official members of his entourage during their 1883 Yellowstone-Jackson Hole tour. (Courtesy NPS, Yellowstone National Park On Line # 09594)

6

PRESIDENT ARTHUR'S TOUR

President Chester A. Arthur's party ...cut a trail down the Gros Ventre into the valley... surveyor W.O. Owen's 1893 map[still] showed a... trail along the Gros Ventre River near the Kelly townsite [a decade after Arthur's party had passed through]. – John Daugherty, *A Place Called Jackson Hole.*

Jackson Hole's reputation for unspoiled wild country and abundant wildlife was becoming well known by the late-nineteenth century. Government-sponsored expedition reports, the creation of nearby Yellowstone National Park, and a return to Nature movement within the United States, were instrumental in informing the country's broader populace of what lay beyond the prairies at places hidden deep within the Rockies.

In 1883, President Chester A. Arthur traveled through the region with a large entourage of Washington officials, dignitaries, guides, and hunters, including seventy-five cavalrymen, and incredibly, 175 pack animals, all at public expense. One writer called it, "the most complete pack train ever organized." Shoshone Chief Washakie, and a frontiersman named Nelson Yarnell, from Fremont County, Wyoming, guided the expedition. [51]

Arthur was originally a New Englander from the mountainous region of Vermont. His father was a Baptist minister and the family lived in a simple clapboard house. Arthur succeeded to the White House from the vice presidency after President James Garfield was assassinated in 1881.

You might say that President Arthur was Jackson Hole's first celebrity tourist. The purpose of his trip was simply recreation. The party entered by way of the old Indian trail from the Upper Green River, crossing Bacon Ridge, and traveling down the Gros Ventre River into Jackson Hole. They cut out and improved the old Indian trail as they went in order to facilitate passage of their imposing cavalcade.[52]

Locally, the route was know as the Bacon Ridge-Gros Ventre trail; it was later dubbed the "Bottle Trail" for the number of cast-off empty bourbon bottles left behind by Arthur's retinue. [53]

From events that followed, we can presume President Arthur's tour, particularly the trail improvements his cavalcade made, indirectly played a role in the progression of Jackson Hole's settlement.

To Jackson Hole

Gros Ventre River

Bacon Ridge

Green River

The Bottle Trail

View from Bacon Ridge down the Gros Ventre River showing the route of the "Bottle Trail" that settlers John Carnes and John Holland followed into Jackson Hole. Mount Moran is in the left background. (Photo by the author)

EURO–AMERICAN SETTLEMENT

7

THE RECOGNIZED FIRST PERMANENT SETTLERS

Jackson's Hole soon became in my eyes, a sort of beatified home for destitute trappers. – William Baillie-Gorhman, 1880.

The early history of Jackson Hole's Euro-American settlement, and that of the settlers themselves, is sketchy and contradictory. One thing is apparent though: settlement of the valley was not at all milk and honey. While we may romanticize it today, in reality it was a rugged and hard-scrabble existence. The Hole's early settlement did not necessarily take place in a manner in which we are generally accustomed to believe the West was won.

In those days, public domain ground was claimed through the exercise of "squatter's rights." A person could "take-up" unclaimed land by staking the corners, building a cabin, making improvements, and living on it. Later, if he/she testified to living there for at least five years, met all the requirements, including making necessary improvements, and had witnesses to collaborate his/her statements in that regard, they could "prove-up;" meaning they could obtain title from the government once the land was surveyed.

In Jackson Hole, there was a hitch, however; the government land surveys required to obtain a homestead patent were not begun until 1892-1893, and then the surveys were limited to a broad determination of section lines within the townships where settlement was concentrated. At best, proving-up for the early settlers in Jackson Hole ended up taking more than a decade.

The principle tools of Jackson Hole's earliest settlers were rifles, traps, and poison – the Winchester Model 73 and 74 repeating rifles, known as "the gun that won the West," and the Sharps rifle, known for its long range and accurate shooting; the Newhouse trap; and strychnine – nothing as benign as the hoe, plow, wagons, family cow, and sun bonnets. All that came much later.

Hunting predatory animals, killing game, and selling hides, trophy heads, and elk tusks, as well as guiding sport hunters, were the grisly sources of most livelihood. This was complimented with summer pasturing of livestock, mostly horses, gathering wild hay, and perhaps, at times, a little gardening. For their lifestyle, a rough-built, two-room cabin, a crude shelter for horses, and maybe some hastily thrown-up corrals initially sufficed as "improvements."

The valley's early settlers occasionally and recklessly lived on both sides of the law; circumstances dictated a do-whatever-was-necessary philosophy. Game laws were basically ignored and rustling some livestock for start-up herds may not have been an out-of-the-question practice. Although picking up a few head of pre-owned cattle was generally considered a minor misdeed, rustling horses was definitely major malfeasance and was not tolerated.

Uinta County, Wyoming, (of which Jackson Hole was a part back then) was about fifty miles wide and 250 miles long. The county seat of Evanston was in the very southwest corner of the state along the

Union Pacific rail line. Jackson Hole was in the most distant reaches of the county's jurisdiction; interference by authorities was rare and unlikely.

Frontiersmen John Holland and John Carnes, along with his common law wife Millie Sorelle, have been labeled "Jackson Hole's founding fathers" by many historians. Millie was the daughter of a Ute Indian and a Euro-American of German descent. Holland, and Carnes and Millie, are generally credited with being "the first to build permanent homesteads" in Jackson Hole. The traditional date given for their settlement is 1884.[54]

That date was a year after Buffalo Bill Cody began his Wild West Show, and the same year that the last herd of wild bison living in the vicinity of Jackson Hole outside Yellowstone National Park was destroyed by commercial hunters. Also, around the time, the last prairie schooner traveled the Oregon Trail. The transcontinental railway had been completed fifteen years earlier. Most of the country's general populace assumed the West was settled by then, but Jackson Hole remained an exception.

The rationale for historians recognizing 1884 as Jackson Hole's settlement date and Carnes and Holland as its first permanent settlers is based upon these two men being the first to bring some type of crude farm machinery into the valley that year. They disassembled the machinery and brought it in with pack horses over the Green River-Bacon Ridge-Gros Ventre trail, following in the trampled-out path of President Arthur's cavalcade the year before – a route into the valley originally established by Native Americans, and later the mountain men. [55]

The apparent conclusion of historians is that bringing in farm machinery demonstrated intent to permanently settle in the valley and cultivate crops. Historian Daugherty declares: "A year after Arthur's tour, settlers [Holland and Carnes] entered Jackson Hole, marking a new era in the valley's history."[56]

Despite this fanciful notion, Holland and Carnes did not simply transport farm equipment, take up homesteads, and begin ranching or farming in a customary manner of events. Like other early denizens of Jackson Hole already mentioned, the two men had been periodically visiting and residing in the valley prior to 1884. There is more intrigue to their story than just "first settlers," however.

Holland and Carnes first became acquainted and friends in the Fontenelle-LaBarge Creek area of the Green River Basin in Wyoming. [57] Historian Fern Nelson called them "trapping buddies, who trapped [together] in Jackson's Hole before 1883."[58] Carnes was about sixteen years older than Holland. Both of them were frequenting the valley long before their recognized date of settlement there. Holland spent time in the Hole in the 1870s[59] and throughout the early 1880s for the catchall purpose of trapping.[60]

By 1883, both men had squatted on land – took up residence without title, as was the practice – immediately northeast of today's Miller Butte on Nowlin Creek, a tributary of the Little Gros Ventre River (today's Flat Creek) in Jackson Hole. That year, Holland filed for water rights from Twin Creek (Curtis Canyon) and Carnes from Flat Creek.[61] Michael Detwiler, who soon became a cattle rancher, also located on Flat Creek, just north of Carnes around this same time, too.[62]

Carnes and Holland were the first to claim water rights in Jackson Hole under Wyoming's territorial law. Securing irrigation rights was a step toward acquiring title to land under the Homestead Act. Both men built typical two-room cabins. The actual date(s) the cabins were constructed is not known; however, their cabins were in existence in1885.[63]

Today, we can hardly comprehend the self-reliance, skills, and labor involved in pioneering within the far-flung Jackson Hole country.

Timber stands, especially those of lodgepole pine (preferred because it grew straight), were a considerable distance from the streamside meadow locations selected by Carnes and Holland for their cabins.

To construct the cabins, they had to fall the trees by hand in the forest, and using their saddle and pack horses, skid the logs a long distance to their respective building sites. There they measured, cut and shaped the timbers, then figured out the means to independently raise the heavy log pieces, ridgepole, and rafters. All this was back-breaking work and without the niceties of nails, glass, door and window frames, or roofing paper.

Since nails were not readily available, everything had to be cut-to-fit or pegged. If any flat-sided timbers were desired, they had to be hand hewn. Inside, an earthen floor was dampened and compacted until it hardened. Sod had to be dug and placed onto the roof to keep out rain and snow; even so, water and mud would likely leak through the roof. The log walls were chinked with willow sticks, mud and moss to keep out the cold air. A blanket hung over the entrance way sufficed for a door. Unless cooking was done outside, a workable fireplace had to be fashioned from native materials at hand; as there was no ready-made cement mix, they made do with clay mud.

But the need for know-how and labor didn't stop there. All food had to be harvested, hunted, or grown on-site; wood for fuel had to be gathered and hauled, cord upon cord, from the forest; all furniture was self-built from local materials, using wooden pegs in place of nails; candles were rendered from elk or deer tallow; and hides were tanned to make or repair moccasins or shoes, clothing, and other leather items. Beyond the distant terminus of the railroad, no one went anywhere faster than a horse could travel.

Fencing to contain horses and any other livestock was generally constructed from lodgepole pine rails and poles. The ground was too rocky in many places, or too frozen at certain times of the year, to dig post holes. Buck-and-rail fence became a signature Jackson Hole feature; barbwire didn't show up until after 1900.

Over-wintering horses and other livestock in the Hole's challenging climate required building a lean-to shelter for them. Then the frontiersman had to somehow cut, generally using nothing more than a butcher knife, and store sufficient wild hay for winter feed. What was called "wild hay" generally consisted of sedge grasses or cottonwood and aspen bark and tips of branchlets. Water was obtained from creeks; even having something as simple as a means to transport water required ingenuity. A building site located near a spring creek that stayed open year-round was a huge advantage; otherwise, a hole had to be chopped through the ice daily. Since warm water was a rarity, bathing was generally an uncommon event.

The list of necessary work and lack of conveniences by today's standards was endless. There was no lace and ruffles in bachelor settler's cabins, but little wonder that they prided themselves on their resourcefulness and self-sufficiency. Despite their rugged existence, and without benefit of modern health care and conveniences, many of Jackson Hole's early settlers lived long and active lives, some into their nineties.

Although any neighbors may have been distant, we can assume that Carnes and Holland interacted with and lived among some singularly

calloused frontier types in those earliest years in Jackson Hole.[64] Lt.
Gustaves Doane's 1876 diary entry stating that the valley "was a
favorite rendezvous for desperadoes and thieves," lends support to
that assumption.[65]

The western frontier was rapidly changing, however. While Carnes
and Holland fit the restless and reckless pattern of the time, as we will
see, in all fairness, they also apparently recognized and enterprisingly
took advantage of the prospects available to them to improve their
lot in life. Both were tough and resourceful frontiersmen; given the
choices they faced while living among hardened outlaws, settling in
Jackson Hole was a thorough test of their mettle.

The improvement of the Green River-Bacon Ridge-Gros Ventre route
into Jackson Hole, wrought by President Arthur's large cavalcade,
was a fortuitous event for Carnes and Holland. They enterprisingly
recognized and capitalized on what a year later was likely still a much
beaten-out trail. It facilitated the transport of their aforementioned
farm machinery and improved the opportunity for trailing livestock
into Jackson Hole from the Upper Green River country. Both men
were already very familiar with the Upper Green from having worked
and resided in the Fontenelle and LaBarge Creek areas, and having
previously traveled the trail from there into Jackson Hole in their
hunting and trapping sorties.

John "Johnny" Carnes Bibliographic Sketch

John Carnes, a twice-wounded Civil War veteran with the Ohio
Volunteer Calvary, was born in Steubenville, Ohio, in 1839. He
reenlisted in 1866 to, as he claimed, "fight Indians." His unit's
principal duty was to guard the Pacific Telegraph's overland route of
communication and supply for military posts. He was also involved
in government construction work, building military posts. Around
1880, Carnes was taken ill while working in the Fontenelle Valley

Portrait of settler John "Johnny" Carnes.
(Courtesy of Jackson Hole Historical Society and Museum 1958.1767.001)

Portrait of settler John H. Holland.
(Courtesy of Jackson Hole Historical Society and Museum 1958.1767.001)

area of the Green River and was nursed by Millie Sorelle.[66] Millie was
the daughter of a Ute Indian woman and trapper of German-French
descent, and the widow of trapper Ike Frappe.[67] She became Carnes'
life partner for forty-three years. Carnes carried mail in the LaBarge
area and homesteaded on Fontenelle Creek of the Green River. He is
reported among the earliest settlers for that area – before 1878.[68] He
relinquished his homestead claim there after moving to Jackson Hole
around 1883. [69]

John H. Holland Biographic Sketch

John H. Holland was born December 14, 1854 in Missouri. [70] His
father, Osham Holland, was from Tennessee, his mother Kentucky. [71]
As a boy and young man, he followed the frontier, moving to Iowa,
then to Kansas, and next to Idaho and Wyoming.[72] Settling and
homesteading in Jackson Hole for more than a decade, he then
moved on to Teton Basin in Idaho where he raised horses, and finally
on to Scio, Oregon, working as a trapper, rancher, hunting guide, and
hotel owner. Historian Fern Nelson describes him as "a fine-looking,
strapping…man who had been a bull-whacker on the construction of
the Oregon Short Line across Wyoming and Idaho …well educated
for the time and place … handy in all pioneering labors;" and who
also played the violin. [73] Holland appears to have demonstrated
enterprising resourcefulness in meeting the demands of frontier life.

According to land-patent records, John Holland made a cash
homestead entry in Franklin County, Idaho, in the Cache Valley, on
April 24, 1879.[74] His presence also in nearby southwest Wyoming
– the LaBarge Creek Valley of the Green River – around that time
is described by historian Nelson and others. [75] Seasonal forays into
Jackson Hole in the late 1870s and early 1880s from both those
locales were readily accomplished.

Portrait of Jackson Hole's most notorious outlaw Teton Jackson.
(Courtesy of Jackson Hole Historical Society and Museum 1958.0003.001p)

8

OUTLAWS, RENEGADES OR LEGITIMATE SETTLERS?

Stock gathered [rustled] throughout Montana and Wyoming were driven over Conant Trail, then south into Pierre's Hole to the Hidden Corrals [along Bitch Creek] or the Teton Basin ... before movement to Utah markets.— Edna Bradford, *Teton Jackson: Life and Times of Jackson Hole's Famous Outlaw.*

Livestock, an item as essential for ranching and homesteading as farm machinery, appears to have been first brought into the Hole by the Green River-Bacon Ridge Trail, too. There is anecdotal and circumstantial evidence that suggests some shenanigans may have been involved in the start-up of the ranching industry in Jackson Hole.

In 1880, there were an estimated 50,000 cattle in the Green River Basin.[76] In 1882, M.E. Post and Francis E. Warren – known as the Spur Outfit – brought another additional 15,000 head of cattle into the Upper Green River valley. Their ranch was located near the mouth of LaBarge Creek and the cattle were run on open range year-round.[77]

One might argue it was purely circumstantial that the Green River Basin happened to be the same area where Holland and Carnes were also residing part of the time. Carnes had taken up a homestead in the Fontenelle and LaBarge Creeks area, Holland in the Cache Valley.

Perhaps, it was only coincidental, but their familiarity with the open-range livestock operations in the Green River Basin, the date cattle first showed up in Jackson Hole, and persistent rumors of rustling being involved, appear to point to more. It suggests they, and perhaps others as well, may have taken advantage of the Spur Outfit's open-range operations to acquire the "start-up" stock necessary for going into the ranching business.

With the large numbers of livestock being run mostly unattended over a vast area, who would notice a few head gone missing? An unwritten rule of the range allowed any unbranded animal over a year old to be claimed and branded by the finder. From the Upper Green River, you would only have needed to push some strays – euphemistically referred to as "picking up extras" – over Bacon Ridge, and then drive them down the Gros Ventre River valley directly into Jackson Hole; as the raven flies, roughly thirty miles – just follow the "Bottle Trail."

Enoch "Cal" Carrington was a young cowboy who met and became friends with John Holland in Teton Basin around 1897; and later, Carrington drifted over into Jackson Hole. [78] Historians Bonney and Bonney refer to him as "a crony of Holland's." [79] In a 1957 interview, Cal revealed the origins of Jackson Hole's early-day ranching industry: "Tim Hibbert and a bunch of them [fellows]…picked up cattle off the Green River Trail and drove them back up in there [to Jackson Hole] for a start. [80] Course, they'd [be] some horses and whenever they got a stray…they pushed him in there, [too]." [81]

Cal did not name who it was that comprised a "bunch of them," however. But various sources based on old Forest Service records indicate there were "one hundred head of cattle in Jackson Hole in 1883, legally-owned by John Holland;" that was the same year Holland filed for his water right in Jackson Hole. [82] All in preparation for settlement, we might presume, and a demonstration of the entrepreneurial nature of frontier enterprise.

In October 1885, seventeen-year-old William "Will" L. Simpson was a wrangler for a posse comprised of sheriffs, deputies and stock association men commanded by Pap Conant.[83] They searched Jackson Hole for a large band of cattle that had "mysteriously vanished from the Wind River country."[84] Simpson later reported: "There were two cabins, which belonged to Carnes and John Holland, his partner, who were trapping in the Jackson Hole country that autumn."[85] Significantly, Carnes and Holland did not identify themselves to the posse as homesteaders or settlers, but rather as "trappers."

Since they were looking for cattle, Conant's posse "made no particular inquiry" about the obviously misappropriated horses they discovered in the Hole – represented by "a great many horse sign," including a band of ponies grazing on Flat Creek meadows and another herd corralled in what was later called Leek's Draw. The proprietors of the pre-owned horse and cow businesses had apparently learned about the posse in advance of their arrival and had skedaddled.[86]

Authorities must have been informed of what Conant's posse had observed though, because in the spring, Federal Marshals corralled William Arnn (note: this was not the Bill Arnn who rode with Butch Cassidy), and questioned him at Malad, Idaho, about who, besides himself, had wintered in Jackson Hole. Considering the valley's earned reputation as an outlaw hideout and Conant's posse's observations, we can speculate that the Marshals were curious who Arnn's neighbors might have been that winter.

According to Arnn's deposition only seven men – himself, John Holland, Robert Miller, Ed Thompson and his partner Hilderbrand, Lock Beye, and Ed Harrington toughed it out in the Hole that

Teton Jackson standing in front of a rough-built frontier cabin with an unidentified person sitting. (from Scribner's magazine, 1904)

winter.[87] It begs the question: where was Carnes? Maybe Arnn simply forgot to mention Carnes, since Pap Conant's posse had identified him as also being present that October.

It stretches the imagination to title this dubious assortment of frontier characters "settlers." Calling them sod-busters or homesteaders to their face more than likely would have produced an amused, wry grin, or perhaps, would have been a dangerous provocation.

Harrington (aka Ed Trafton) had a reputation as a thief. He had already been busted once in 1881 for rustling by Sam Swanner, a Blackfoot, Idaho, law officer; and he had also had a run-in with Hiram Lapham in Teton Basin for rustling the Lapham's livestock.[88]

Named "the most underrated holdup man in the Old West" by his grandson John Watson, in *The Real Virginian*, Harrington was born Edwin B. Trafton in 1857 in New Brunswick, Canada, to immigrant parents. His father died when Ed was nine years old. Romanticized tales of outlaws Frank and Jesse James and the Younger brothers stirred young Trafton's imagination; his entire life he tried to emulate his infamous post-civil war heroes. At an early age, he left home and headed west for the territories. Convicted of petty theft, he ended up in the Denver Home for Delinquent Boys. Sometime after his release, he stole forty dollars and a favorite horse from his mother and lit out again, this time for the gold fields in the Black Hills of South Dakota.

Disillusioned by the hard labor involved, Trafton lost interest in gold mining, deciding instead to seek fame and fortune by other means on the Western frontier. He drifted into Teton Basin around 1878 or '80 and took up squatter's rights in the northern part of the valley. Assuming the alias, Harrington, he and his associates poached game in Yellowstone National park and preyed on livestock owners within the region. Rustling horses and cattle, they drove them across the

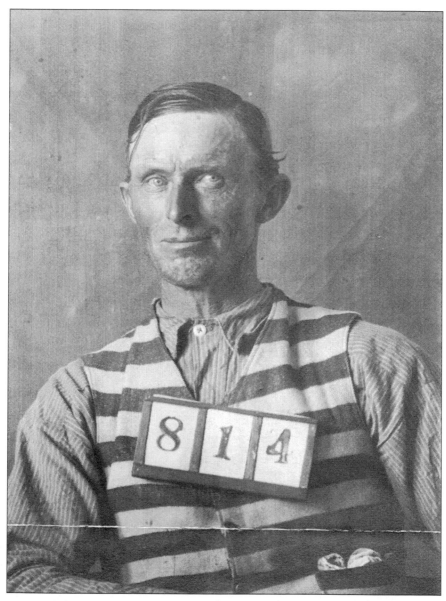

Ed Harrington (aka Edwin B. Trafton) at the Idaho Penitentiary in 1901.
(Courtesy Idaho State Historical Society)

mountains into Jackson Hole and south into Utah. Watson records, "Farmers bought the livestock little concerned about where it came from as long as they got a bill of sale proving they hadn't done the stealing."

In between arrests in 1881, 1887 and 1901, and serious jail time, Harrington appeared to be a respectable citizen to most of his Teton Basin neighbors, serving as a mail carrier, hunting guide, and to the homesteaders' wives, "someone who liked to sing and dance." He built and maintained a lakeside squatter's cabin at Colter Bay in Jackson Hole. In 1914, he gained national notoriety by holding up fifteen stagecoaches in one afternoon in Yellowstone National Park. As a consequence, soon after, Harrington graduated to Leavenworth Penitentiary.

Thompson and his partner, Hilderbrand, were proven rascals, compadres of outlaw Teton Jackson (aka William Bradford, Harvey Gleason). Thompson and Teton Jackson, had been implicated earlier in the horrific Cooper killing at Badger Creek in Teton Basin.[89] At the time, however, Teton Jackson, "Jackson Hole's most notorious outlaw," was cooling off in the Boise Penitentiary for grand larceny – a fancy way of saying horse stealing.[90]

Teton Jackson was a product of the violent aftermath of the Civil War. He was born in Massachusetts around 1846, and his family moved to Missouri. In a desire for adventure and independence, he ran away at age nineteen. He joined up with the gangs of young militants in "bloody Missouri," a time and place where some of country's renowned outlaws were produced. After a fracas with the law, he headed west, reportedly first arriving in Jackson Hole sometime around or after 1865.[91]

Teton Jackson, according to some, led the "toughest gang that ever infested the Rocky Mountains."[92] Conversely, others declare that fact an "exaggeration," saying, Teton Jackson was really "an accommodating fellow, a good singer, and had many friends."[93] More likely, that came later after his retirement to Lander, Wyoming, where he began operating "a hunting guide business."[94]

In any case, in the spring of 1885 or 86, Teton Jackson escaped from prison. His gang's "log fortress" had been strategically located at the south-end of Miller Butte in Jackson Hole in 1877.[95] It was surrounded by swampy ground and Jackson claimed, "It could defeat against anything except artillery."[96]

Teton Jackson reportedly told W.E. Hosford, a Wyoming stock detective, that "his gang numbered up to ten men … and that they obtained their supplies from two men residing in the Hole named Carnes and Holland."[97] Carnes, Holland, and Robert Miller were also suspect by the association established through Arnn's testimony mentioned earlier, that is, they were among the seven men, including members of Teton Jackson's gang, who had over wintered together in Jackson Hole.

A legend also tells of Teton Jackson's right-hand man, Thompson, being "en route to Carnes' cabin" to get John's help in replacing a rifle sight, when he encountered some lawmen. Thompson stood them off in a shootout from a rock outcrop on Miller Butte, known thereafter as "Fort Standoff."[98] The tale suggests Carnes and Thompson may have been downright neighborly with one another.

Other anecdotes point to Holland's possible culpability. Holding corrals once existed at the head of Flat Creek Canyon in Jackson Hole. Cal Carrington, in interview decades later, claimed: "It was where outlaws had hid their stolen horses."[99] It is commonly rumored Carrington had hid stolen horses there, too. But, more to fact, Jackson old-timer Charlie Petersen, early settler Frank Petersen's son, said that "Carrington had told him it was Holland who had originally built the corrals."[100]

It is reported that Robert Miller hunted and trapped in Jackson Hole beginning around 1883; he then left, but returned a year or two later flush with money, which according to hearsay, may have been "dishonestly obtained."[101] If true, he wisely remained closemouthed about his stash. He filed for a water right from Cache Creek in 1884, and the next year brought the first wagon into the valley over Teton Pass, indicating he had something more permanent in mind than following the outlaw trail.

In all fairness, Carnes, Holland, and Miller did not have a choice of neighbors. Out of necessity, they did what the times required. The unwritten rule was that you did not ask a man about his business, nor did he inquire about yours. Although they may have been suspected of rustling and being accomplices in Teton Jackson's pre-owned stock business, it was never proven.

Author Nollie Mumey summed it up: "It was difficult to know who was in league with outlaws [back then], for many times men who appeared to be honest and trustworthy, were actually [or had been] associated with the thieves."[102] In any case, one must agree, "it was a rough crew that first settled Jackson Hole."[103]

Later, through interviews with outlaw Ed Harrington, novelist Owen Wister gained keen insight into those early days, writing in his 1902 western classic, *The Virginian*: "Somewhere at the eastern base of the Tetons did those hoof prints disappear into a mountain sanctuary where many crooked paths have led. He that took another man's possessions or…another man's life, could always run here… [where] there skulked a nomadic and distrustful population. This in due time built cabins, took wives, begat children and came to speak of itself as 'the honest settlers of Jackson's Hole.'"[104]

Unknown hunter's cabin near Moran, Wyoming, with bear and cougar hides and elk and moose antlers.

(Courtesy of Jackson Hole Historical Society and Museum 1958.0993.001p)

9

A SETTLEMENT PROUDLY LACKING IN DECORUM

When the United States Army took over the administration of Yellowstone National Park in 1886, the trappers and poachers were booted out of the park. They scattered and it was in this year that most of the trappers moved to the Jackson Hole country to the south. – Grace Johnson, *Colter's Hell.*

In 1892, when historian Fredrick Jackson proclaimed the American frontier "finally closed," conditions surrounding the rugged Teton Mountains did not agree. Surveyor William Owen, that same year, described the Teton area as "rugged and wild beyond the power of words to convey."[105]

Sometime around 1885, it is thought that Robert Miller bought Teton Jackson's squatter's claim and the log buildings comprising the outlaw's "fortress." If true, perhaps Teton-Jackson did have an "accommodating" side as was mentioned earlier. In Miller's 1894 homestead application, he testified that he "built his house in 1885." No doubt it was the one-room, dirt-floor outlaw cabin he had acquired.

Possibly using what was known as a "Mormon brake" – dragging a large log or tree behind the wagon to slow it down – Miller brought a wagon into Jackson Hole over Teton Pass in 1885, and later, a horse-drawn mowing machine, too. Or he may have disassembled the wagon and machinery and horse-packed them across the pass. He had undoubtedly obtained the items through the railhead and Mormon communities at Rexburg or St. Anthony, Idaho.

Miller traveled back East and married Grace Green in 1893, and together they took up residence in Jackson Hole. By 1895, they were running 126 cattle, and not too long after, up to 500 head.[106] The Millers are credited with being "pioneers with vision."[107] They built their home – an extravagant residence for the time that took two years to complete – on the ground believed to have been the location of Teton Jackson's fortress hideout which Miller purchased earlier. Some recognize Robert Miller as being the "first life-long resident of Jackson Hole." Today, the Miller's original log home is preserved on the National Elk Refuge and is listed on the National Register of Historic Places.

Regardless of the impression of lawlessness in those early years, John Holland is also credited with a list of legitimate pursuits. He was the first bachelor settler in Jackson Hole to have a garden; served as a mail carrier across Teton Pass; financed the start up of Don Driggs' mercantile store in the settlement of Driggs, Idaho; and dug some of the original irrigation ditches in Jackson Hole which are still in use today.[108] Carnes must have attempted to put the farm machinery they horse-packed-in to use, too, for he is credited with being "the first to farm in Jackson Hole."

Besides his small cabin and outbuildings, Holland also testified in his 1894 Homestead Pre-Emption Proof that he had built "one-and-one-half miles of irrigating ditches."[109] Ditches were named after their owners and "Holland Ditch #1" is still in use today, diverting water to 160-acres of pasture in the Flat Creek area on the National Elk Refuge.[110]
By 1888, within four to five years after Carnes and Holland are

considered to have taken up permanent residence, the valley had collected a rapidly growing population of pioneers; a total of about twenty men, two women, and one child were living in Jackson Hole. Berthe Nelson was the second woman to take up residence (after Millie Sorelle) and her daughter Cora, the first child. However, the settlement remained dominated by bachelors until the twentieth century. In his published *Recollections*, Thomas E. Crawford, who came into the Hole in 1888, described the residents of this time period as: "homeless, reckless, straight-shooting and hard drinking."

These early settlers or "bachelor trappers" as they were apt to characterize themselves, were an eccentric and colorful lot. They arrived in the valley either around the same time or right-on-the-heels of Carnes, Holland, and Miller, and some were here even before. They included, among others: William Arnn, John Cherry, William Crawford, T.E. Crawford, J. P. Cunningham, "Uncle Jack" Davis, Mike Detweiler, Moses "Mose" Giltner, Jack Hicks, Stephen Leek, William "Old Bill" Manning, Martin "Sloughgrass" Nelson, John Pierce, John "Jack" Shive, Dick Turpin, Frank Wood, Emil Wolff, and "Old Puzzle Face," said to be a "fugitive from justice," as were Jack Davis and Dick Turpin, too. [111]

William Arnn, mentioned earlier, was living year-round in the Hole by 1884; Mike Detweiler had taken up squatter's rights in the valley by that time, too, and reportedly, was running one of the Hole's earliest cattle herds. Detweiler eventually sold his homestead claim to Robert Miller. John Pierce, assuming it is the same Pierce that Lt. Doane recorded to be living in a crude cabin at South Park, would have been residing in the valley since the winter of 1876.

Dick Turpin (aka Richard Smalley), a colorful, fiery-tempered, bushy-bearded bachelor was among those early settlers seeking to put distance between themselves and the law – rumor was he had killed a

Settlers Dick Turpin (left) and Frank Petersen trapped together in the Gros Ventre in the 1880s.
(Courtesy of Jackson Hole Historical Society and Museum 1958.0340.001p)

man in a knife fight. Born in 1840 in Ohio, Turpin was a Civil War veteran who served with the Union Army, and worked as a civilian bull-train freighter for the military. He may have come into the valley "to trap" as early as 1880, although some sources say it was 1887. He located at a hidden-away place, the Red Hills in the Gros Ventre River valley. Settler Frank Petersen reportedly trapped with Turpin at Goose Creek in the Gros Ventre in 1889.[112] Dick eventually moved out of the Gros Ventre valley and took-up squatter's rights just north of today's town site of Jackson. Turpin Meadow in Buffalo Valley and Turpin Creek, a tributary of the Gros Ventre River, were named after him.

What name was rightfully his, Turpin or Smalley, remains a favorite unresolved question among Jackson Holers. If the name Turpin was an alias, he may have borrowed the moniker from the infamous highway robber, "Dick Turpin," an Englishman executed as a horse thief in 1739, whose exploits were popularly romanticized in ballads and theater in the nineteenth century. If true, it leaves an impression Richard Smalley harbored a certain pride in his reputation for unruliness.

> Three hundred guineas on Turpin's head,
> trap him alive or shoot him dead ...
> Out of the stable, a wave of thunder, swept Black Bess ...
> He leaped to the saddle, and ... was gone ...
> And the hunted self was like a cloud;
> but the hunter like the wind...
> [and at] the gates of hell...
> stretched out a ghostly hand... stained with blood
> "Welcome," it said,
> Thou'st ridden well, and outstripped all but me. [113]

– Lines from "The Ballad of Dick Turpin" by Alfred Noyes

Fitting Jackson Hole's pattern of frontiersmen turned settler, Emil Wolff had been a member of one the early Yellowstone Expeditions,

Early Jackson Hole settler John Cherry in his skinning apron displaying his catch of otter and lynx pelts at his cabin.
(Courtesy of Jackson Hole Historical Society and Museum 1958.2617.001)

most likely Doane's.[114] In the mid-1880s, he was stationed with the U.S. Army at Fort Hall. After being discharged, he moved to Pierre's Hole in 1886; a year or two later he abandoned his squatter's claim there, and moved over the pass to Jackson Hole, settling on Flat Creek.[115] In 1895, Wolff pulled up stakes and moved again, this time settling north of Spread Creek (just north of today's Triangle X Ranch) in the northern part of the valley.[116] Years later, Wolff's son, "Stippy," said what precipitated the move to Spread Creek was that Emil had consistently observed "herds of thousands of elk and antelope" on the meadows in that area.[117] By the late1890s, Wolff was reported to own seventy-five head of cattle, but like many at the time, he also began guiding sport hunters as his principle source of income.[118] The Wolff Irrigation Ditch in the north-end of the valley is named after him.

A renowned colorful character, settler John Cherry is said to have "lived a rugged, free lifestyle." Known for his outrageous tales, separating the facts from his mistruths becomes difficult. Born around 1853 in Tennessee, his parents moved to the Median River Valley in Texas, where his father fought against the Comanche Indians and served in the Mexican War. At age eleven, John left home. An illiterate orphan, he signed his name with an X his entire life. He was befriended by the celebrated cattle drover Jesse Chisholm and worked on one of Chisholm's cattle drives to Abilene, Kansas.

Cherry always insisted his brother was the notorious Nebraska horse thief Doc Middleton. John found his way to Laramie, where he reportedly worked as an Army scout, guide, and trapper. He drifted into Jackson Hole in 1887 and took up squatter's rights at Warm Springs, four miles north of today's town site of Jackson. The remnants of his homestead cabin are still there. In Jackson Hole, he trapped and guided sport hunters – his specialty was hunting mountain lion and bear using hounds. It is said he maintained his

Settler Roy McBride proudly displays six wolf hides. The bounty money he collected for killing the six wolves easily exceeded a year's worth of wages. (Courtesy of Jackson Hole Historical Society and Museum 1958.1784.1)

hunting hounds by feeding them elk. John ranched a little too – he had thirteen cattle in 1895 – but became best known for racing horses. In later years, he worked as a wrangler for the Bar BC dude ranch. John played the fiddle, but only knew one tune. He was said to be generally "friendly and talkative, but could be rather wild looking."[119]

John S. "Jack" Shive's frontier background was also characteristic of the Hole's earliest settlers. Born in 1862 on a farm near Philadelphia, he reportedly didn't get along with his father, who was said to be cruel. At age fourteen Jack ran away from home. A few years later, he joined the U.S. Army and was sent to Montana, where he served with the First Calvary. His regiment saw action against the Crow Indians. Later he was among the Army personnel assigned to the administration of Yellowstone National Park. In 1891, after being discharged from the Army, he built a small cabin along the Snake River, just south of Yellowstone Park, and spent the winter there. Next, he moved further south, to the willow flats in Buffalo Valley, where he took up squatter's rights and built a one-room homestead cabin.

Contrary to most bachelor settler's reputations for wretched housekeeping, military spit-and-polish had rubbed-off on Jack; reportedly he kept his cabin "as neat and shining as a new pin." Said to be "a man of few words," Shive was the first settler to take up land in the far-removed northern part of Jackson Hole.[120] To travel from the northern part of the Hole to its southern end generally required a two-day trip by horseback back then.

In October 1889, the Mormon families of Elijah "Uncle Nick" Wilson, Sylvester Wilson, and Selar Cheney arrived over Teton Pass with six covered wagons to take up residence in Jackson Hole. They improved the Teton Pass route into Jackson Hole as they went, upgrading the steep trail for passage of their wagons – a near impossible feat at the time. While Robert Miller had managed to

Traveling the narrow Teton Pass road by horse drawn wagon in summer. Elk poacher Binkley's wife and children hauled two wagon loads of goods (mostly elk hides and antlers) out over Teton Pass to the railhead at St. Anthony in this manner (see page 151).

(Courtesy of Jackson Hole Historical Society and Museum 191.40461) wrestle a wagon over the pass in 1885, the Wilson-Cheney party further opened the way for settlement, proving the pass was a feasible, but difficult, wagon route.

The Wilson-Cheney families found themselves in a dire circumstance after descending into the Hole; they had arrived too late in the season to build cabins. Already established settlers had to help the hard-pressed new arrivals. They avoided tragic consequences through residents Carnes, Holland, and John Cherry providing them with temporary quarters.

In addition to his original two-room cabin, Carnes had later built a larger three-room house. Millie and John Carnes gave Sylvester, Mary, and Nick Wilson a place to live by letting them use their old, original sod-roof cabin. Similarly, Holland let Selar Cheney and his family move into his two-room cabin.[121]

John Cherry allowed late arrivals Ervin and Mary Jane Wilson, along with their six-week old baby, to use his homestead and cabin located at Warm Springs, just north of Gros Ventre Butte. In a memoir, Mary Jane Wilson wrote, "we lived that first winter on elk meat and water gravy…the snow lay on the ground till May."[122] Their two cows did not make it through the winter.[123]

The new settlers celebrated their first Christmas at bachelor settler Will Crawford's place, during which, Holland, along with the others, played the violin and danced. Holland also supplied the new arrivals with hay. Robert Miller is reported to have given them hay, too, requiring one and a half tons to be paid back for every ton loaned.[124] Carnes showed them how to make moccasins. That spring, the Mormon families gathered for Jackson Hole's first Easter Services, held at Holland's homestead.[125]

Similarly, in 1896, the newly arrived Budge, Allen and May families temporarily used Holland and Carnes cabins while building their own.[126] The uses of property – cabins, stables, and hay – were likely not offered out of free-hearted neighborliness alone; we can assume it involved some exchange of favors or payment. During those times, the homesteads owners (Carnes, Cherry, and Holland) either temporarily moved elsewhere in Jackson Hole or left the valley.

Mormon settlers brought families and domesticity with them. Except for the practice of polygamy, they were generally law-abiding people. They located, not on widely-scattered homesteads, but instead banded together into close communities – Wilson, Kelly, Grovont (which became known as Mormon Row). The Grovont settlement location boasted some of the better, deeper soil in the valley. The top soil there was comprised of up to twelve-foot deep alluvial outwash from Ditch Creek.

While some Mormon settlers ranched, many tended to be farmers: grubbing-up the sagebrush, plowing the prairie, planting grain, particularly "90-day oats," harvesting wild hay, cultivating gardens (root vegetables such as carrots, beets and rutabagas did best), running a few cows, and keeping laying hens; a far different lifestyle than the Hole's bachelor settlers.

A word about farming in the Hole: those who tried it exclusively generally ended up in financial trouble. Author and dude rancher Burt Struthers, in *The Diary of a Dude Rancher*, attributed the economic problems of the valley in 1924 to settlers who attempted "to suit the country to themselves, rather than suiting themselves to the country." In Struther's opinion, cattle ranching proved to be the only suitable agricultural enterprise for the valley. Because of the short, unpredictable growing season – at most, sixty frost-free days – and distances to market, even hard-working farmers were simply unable to make a living. By the late 1920s, the list of property owners owing back taxes who had attempted to rely on farming for a living was prophetically and badly out-of-hand.[127]

In 1892, the first post office was established in Jackson Hole on Fred White's homestead, just north of today's fish hatchery on the National Elk Refuge. It was named Marysvale after White's wife Mary. The post office itself consisted of a canvas-covered wagon box.[128] It served as Jackson's Hole's only mailing address for several years. Later, the post office was moved to Cache Creek at Maggie Simpson's homestead and she would call it Jackson. Simpson's homestead was located about where Cache Creek crosses under today's Redmond Street in Jackson.

Early-day settler Frank Petersen's Jackson Hole developed homestead in 1917 located near Poverty Flats just south of Marysvale.
(Courtesy of Rena Croft)

10
A SAMPLING OF EARLY SETTLER BIOGRAPHIES

There has not been a report to his office of any horse stealing or of any other unlawful act [in Jackson Hole]...since 1892 [when] two noted desperadoes were arrested [shot down] for horse stealing... There is no better class of citizens in any place in the state than those who have made their homes in the beautiful region known as Jackson's Hole. – John Ward, Uinta County Sheriff, 1895.

Life histories of four prominent early day Jackson Hole settlers are profiled here. The original settlers typically shared similar backgrounds. Most had a history of leaving Midwestern homes at an early age and roaming the frontier before settling. Along the way, they worked whatever jobs were offered: the Union Pacific Railroad, the U.S. Army, cattle ranches, livestock yards, as teamsters, and especially hunting and trapping – from buffalo and commercial meat and hide hunting to trapping furbearers and killing large predators for bounties and guiding sport hunters.

Frequently, they claimed to have originally wandered into Jackson Hole for the purpose of hunting and trapping. Often the men were Civil War veterans or their lives had somehow been directly disrupted by the war. A few were hiding from the law and looking to get a new start. The parents of many had been immigrants to the United States.

Portrait of early settler Moses "Mose" V. Giltner.
(Courtesy of Jackson Hole Historical Society and Museum 1958.0199.001p)

All of the settlers demonstrated a rugged adaptability, toughness, resourcefulness, a strong sense of individuality, and possessed the necessary skills and knowledge for survival on the frontier. These essentials included horsemanship and horse packing, cabin construction, hunting, trapping, making one's own clothing and leather repairs, and otherwise living independently off the land.

Driven by the restless American pioneering spirit, they all held one ambition in common: to move on to new land and places, always looking for and seeking new and better opportunities. In so doing, they played a predestined role in America's expansionist movement known as Manifest Destiny.

Moses "Mose" V. Giltner[129]

Moses Giltner was an enterprising and hard-working pioneer, eventually developing his homestead into one of the most successful ranches in Jackson Hole. Born in Nodaway County, Missouri, in 1857, Giltner was the third of seven children. His father was a farmer who served in the Union Army during the Civil War, while his family was subjected to the war's ravages.

Leaving home as a young man, after a family dispute, Moses traveled and resided for awhile in Washington Territory, where he prospected for gold. After drifting about on the frontier in the Northwest, he eventually settled in Wyoming. Giltner claimed when he arrived in Jackson Hole in 1886, he was one of twenty-two bachelor settlers. In 1889, he built a cabin on Spring Creek, where he vigorously developed a ranch out of raw land, eventually increasing it to 320 acres.

In 1898, he further increased his land holdings by purchasing "Slough Grass" Nelson's 160-acre homestead on Flat Creek, which he then attempted to drain using a dredge. Becoming one of the valley's leading farmers and largest cattle ranchers, his herd consisted of forty-five cows in 1895; by 1910, he owned 301 head. His crops consisted mostly of timothy, alfalfa, wild hay, and some grain.

Giltner rode with the posse that shot and killed the two alleged horse rustlers at the Cunningham Ranch in 1892. His cryptic, but honest, comment afterward was: "I was a damned fool to have ever gotten involved … it was just plain murder." Giltner was also a member of Constable Manning's posse in Jackson Hole's Indian War of 1895.

Giltner was a citizen of influence and progressive ideas. In 1905, the first telephone line in Jackson Hole was strung between the Jackson Hotel and Giltner's Ranch, a distance of three miles. People in Jackson took turns talking to Moses on the phone from the hotel. He had one of the first automobiles in Jackson Hole, a 1917 Buick Four, which he brought in over Teton Pass.

In his old age, Giltner, not unlike many of Jackson Hole's confirmed bachelors, was considered an eccentric character by newer arrivals. One local called him "downright odd," because allegedly he would wear rubber overshoes over his boots all the time, regardless of the weather. His questionable house-cleaning habits and a lack of personal hygiene in his latter years made him the subject of local gossip and yarns. Giltner, it was joked, would travel all the way to Lava Hot Springs, Idaho, for his annual bath.

Bachelor settler John Cherry and Moses were good friends. During Cherry's last years, he boarded with Giltner. The two old timers looked out for each other. When Cherry died in St. John's Hospital in Jackson in 1931, he left Giltner his horses, including his prized stallion. Giltner found a local young rider, Johnny Ryan, to jockey for him, and became known for racing horses at rodeos.

Moses Giltner died in 1941 and was buried in Jackson's Aspen Hill Cemetery. His headstone inscription reads: "A Rugged Pioneer."

William "Old Bill" F. Manning[130]

William "Bill" Manning was an archetype of those who pioneered America's westward movement. Born in Allen County, Ohio, on March 7, 1836, he was orphaned at age two when his mother died. His father had fought in the War of 1812. Bill enlisted under the Union flag in 1861 and served with the 57th Ohio Infantry. Reportedly, he survived fighting at Shiloh, Gettysburg, and battles around Richmond, rising to the rank of Captain.

In 1866, he tried settling in Iowa, then moved to Kansas, next to Colorado, and then Texas, working as a blacksmith and buffalo hunter. In 1872, he enlisted again, this time with the 5th U.S. Infantry; part of the enlistment was spent at Fort Leavenworth, Kansas, fighting Indians under the command of General Nelson Miles.

From 1879 through 1891, he engaged in mining and hunting in Montana, Colorado, Teton Basin, Idaho, and reportedly, withinYellowstone National Park, too, after which he settled in South Park in Jackson Hole.

As a young man, Manning was an imposing or commanding figure. He reportedly was tall, well-over six-feet in height, with a large drooping mustache; he wore a large western hat and high-heeled riding boots. In 1894, he was elected Jackson Hole's constable and took it upon himself to: "break up the predatory habits of the Indians and prevent them from roaming over the public domain at will, hunting wherever they chose, wantonly slaughtering elk."

In 1895, recruiting deputies from the local citizenry, and with the support of Jackson Hole's Justice of the Peace Frank H. Rhodes and

Portrait of William F. "Old Bill" Manning.
(Courtesy Jackson Hole Historical Society and Museum 1958.0199.001 p)

Wyoming Governor, William A. Richards, Constable Manning, along with his special deputies, sought out, confronted, and arrested Indians they encountered within the Jackson Hole area. In one incident, they shot and killed a peaceful Indian and wounded another. Manning's actions were widely castigated by Easterners and declared to be lawless murder, but in the end he was sustained by the Supreme Court of the United States.

Manning's actions were controversial. Seven years later, a critic wrote in *Outdoor Life* about Manning's ironic failure to enforce the game laws among his own fellow whites: "…bumptious Bill has been sucking the public teat for many seasons, giving nothing but evil for the good money he has received." Manning was also known for his outspoken disapproval of the establishment of Teton Park and was totally against all legislation for land set-asides that removed lands from the local tax rolls. He did have his supporters, though. One account stated: "Mr. Manning is a thorough frontiersman, skilled in all exigencies and ways of the wilderness, having learned them by practice through years of danger, privation, and arduous toil."

William Manning lived a long and active life; at age 94 he applied for the job of mail carrier in Jackson Hole. He died on August 14, 1932, after forty-two days of fighting illness. The "grand old frontiersman," as he was called, was oldest resident in Jackson Hole at the time. He was given a military funeral and buried in South Park Cemetery in Jackson Hole.

Robert "Bobby" E. Miller[131]

Historian's have called Robert Miller "a pioneer with vision." A controversial and shrewd businessman, he was born in Argyle, Wisconsin, in 1863, to Scottish immigrant parents. At age seventeen, Miller got a job at a bank in Illinois; at nineteen, he worked on the Union Pacific Railroad at Sidney, Nebraska. His next move was to

Portrait of early settler Robert "Bobby" Miller in his Forest Service uniform.
(Courtesy USDA Forest Service)

Denver, where he again worked in a bank, after which, he drifted up to Montana, passing through Jackson Hole around 1883 or 1884, reportedly "trapping."

Returning to Jackson Hole a year later, Miller selected the same ground for a homestead that the notorious outlaw Teton Jackson and his gang had occupied. It is said he bought the squatter rights and a cabin from the outlaws for twenty-five dollars.

Enterprising and energetic, Miller was the first to bring a wagon over Teton Pass in 1885; and later, a mowing machine, too. He labored at developing his homestead, while trapping in winters.

In 1892, Miller rode with the posse that killed the two alleged rustlers at the Cunningham Ranch cabin; after that episode, he was appointed Jackson Hole's first Constable by Uinta County Commissioners.

In 1893, he traveled to Ottawa, Illinois, to marry Grace Green. It is rumored, she, like Robert, also arrived in Jackson Hole with money. In 1895, the Millers built what was considered a "lavish" six-bedroom home (listed today on the National Register of Historic Places). In 1895, they had 126 cattle; by 1905, their herd had grown to more than 400 head. Through purchase of adjacent homesteads, the Millers greatly expanded their ranch lands, becoming the largest ranch in Jackson Hole. Writer and photographer Frederic Irland, who met Miller in 1903, wrote: "Robert Miller...represents the best type of Western ranchman."

Serving as a U.S. Commissioner, Miller certified statements on settlers' homestead applications. In 1902, he was appointed supervisor of the Teton Division of the Forest Reserve, and in 1908, Forest Supervisor for the Teton National Forest, a position he held for a decade. In this capacity, Miller was involved in efforts to indict the notorious elk tuskers operating in the Jackson Hole area. In 1914, he started the Jackson State Bank. Miller is often remembered for his hard-nosed business dealings and making bitter foreclosures as a banker. He earned the nick name "Old Twelve Percent," for the loan interest he charged.

The Millers moved into the town of Jackson after the federal government bought their 1,760-acre ranch to start the National Elk Refuge in 1915. Around 1928, Miller was hired as the purchasing agent for Rockefeller's controversial Snake River Land Company, buying up properties that would eventually become Grand Teton National Park. He later denied knowledge of the land company's intended purpose.

While working in his garden in 1934, Miller suffered a fatal heart attack. Buried in Ottawa, Illinois, a large crowd of mourners reportedly followed behind his casket as it left Jackson. Miller Butte north of Jackson is named after him.

Frank L. Petersen[132]

A well known and respected early day Jackson Hole citizen, Frank Petersen was born in Kobelev, Denmark in 1860; the fifth child in a family of nine. At age seventeen, Frank made two trips across the Atlantic to the United States, caring for livestock being transported by steamship. Several of Frank's siblings had already immigrated to the United States, settling in Iowa and Nevada.

After the last livestock run, Frank followed his siblings to Iowa, working in a nearby meat packing plant. Lured by tales from cowboys arriving with cattle at the packing plant, he headed west, working on ranches in South Dakota and Wyoming.

In 1889, Petersen first visited Jackson Hole on a hunting trip and trapped with settler Dick Turpin at Goose Creek in the Gros Ventre. Dick Turpin was living at the Red Hills in the Gros Ventre at the time. That spring, Petersen took up a homestead along Flat Creek, just south of Marysvale at a place known as Poverty Flats.

Besides ranching, Frank made his living as a guide and by trapping. Hunting clients back then would stay for four to six weeks. They were picked up at the railheads at either Livingston or Gardiner, Montana, or St. Anthony, Idaho, and then transported to Jackson Hole by wagon or saddle horse.

As early as 1895, Frank was advertising his guiding services in *Recreation Magazine*:

FRANK PETERSEN
Mountaineer and Guide
Takes Out Hunting Parties
And Tourists to Yellowstone Park.
Prices to Suit the Times.
ADDRESS,
Marysvale, Uinta Co., Wyoming

The routes and difficulties encountered for hunting parties traveling to Jackson Hole were vividly recalled by one of Petersen's clients, Frederic Irland, in a 1903 *Scribner's Magazine* article entitled, "The Wyoming Game Stronghold." Irland first tried to reach Jackson Hole by horseback from Rawlins by way of Togwotee Pass and was turned back by snow. He went back to Rawlins and traveled on by rail to St. Anthony, finally managing to cross Teton Pass with his horses floundering in the deep snow. With Irland, Frank guided perhaps the first person seeking to only photograph wildlife in Jackson Hole, not shoot it.

Portrait of early settler Frank L. Petersen. (Courtesy of Rena Croft)

After Petersen had a seven-room log home built, he used his original two-room homestead cabin for a bunkhouse. At the same time, he worked at developing his ranch, constructing irrigation ditches, fencing, barns, and corrals. Like many, Petersen's family also relied on game meat for subsistence. Frank was also known for keeping a small band of elk in an enclosure next to his home, some of which were sold for restoration programs in Pennsylvania and other states. Irland reported Frank had a dozen elk in the enclosure in 1903.

Petersen was also a posse member at the 1892 Cunningham Ranch shootout, where the two alleged horse rustlers were killed. He climbed the Grand Teton with the 1898 William Owen mountaineering party, pioneering what today is known as the "Owen-Spalding route;" and, he also rode with Manning's posse in the Indian War of 1895.

In 1899, Petersen acquired a "starter herd" of two cows. A decade later he had grown his herd to more than a hundred head. In 1905, Frank courted and married Rena J. Peterson (with a "son," his was "sen"), who was from Teton Basin. At the time, Rena was living in Jackson, working for Grace Miller for "four dollars a week, room and board." Frank and Rena were married in Driggs, Idaho. It took them eleven days to make the return trip back over the pass.

Petersen was one of the contractors that conducted a log drive on the Snake to provide timbers to build a bridge near Menor's Ferry at Moose, Wyoming. Frank was community-minded and belonged to civic and fraternal organizations, including the "Jackson Hole Gun and Commercial Club" and the Odd Fellows. As Jackson grew, he served as a game warden, tax assessor (conducted in winter on skis), county deputy sheriff, and county commissioner. Frank Petersen died September 11, 1929. He is buried in Jackson's Aspen Hill Cemetery over looking the valley.

Montana rancher and grazing association regulator, John Chapman, whose horses were reclaimed
at Jackson Hole's Cunningham Ranch after two alleged horse thieves were gunned down.
(Courtesy of Montana Historical Society Research Center, Helena, Montana)

11
JACKSON HOLE'S CUNNINGHAM RANCH INCIDENT

"1000 STOLEN HORSES IN JACKSON HOLE
Stockmen on Their Way after Them

The rendezvous for the horse thieves has been at Jackson's Hole, a basin near Yellowstone Park in Wyoming. There are now congregated there, according to reports, from fifteen to twenty rustlers, and they have in their possession about 1,000 head of stolen horses ... The [Montana] cattle and horse companies are credited with having raised a large fund...to exterminate rustlers and they have employed the bravest men they can find...who can shoot as well as they can ride. They are paid $1000 for their services..." – April 6, 1892, Helena, Montana's Daily Independent newspaper.

The *Daily Independent's* hyperbolized reporting was not entirely untrue. The April 1892 incident looms large in Jackson Hole's history. Carnes, Holland, Miller, Giltner, Petersen, and other early Jackson Hole settlers were participants on the side of the law, but "the law," as it turned out, in this case, was a shadowy entity.

At the time, ranchers in Montana and Wyoming were suffering large losses due to rustling. Fed up, Montana stock growers organized to exterminate "the rustling scourge" once and for all. Jackson Hole settlers were unaware, and were unknowingly recruited – without proper lawful authority – to participate in a part of the Montana stockmen's dragnet.[133]

Stolen horses had been tracked to Jackson Hole in 1891, but winter's snow had already closed Teton Pass, preventing their recovery. In April 1892, Montana grazing association regulator and rancher, John Chapman, rancher W.J. Anderson, and hired regulator Sim "Slick" Roberts, posing as law officers with the authority to act through the engagement of citizens from Uinta County, Wyoming (Teton County hadn't been formed yet), showed up in Teton Basin, Idaho, and enlisted John Holland to lead them across Teton Pass on snowshoes.[134] Holland was appointed "special deputy." Once on the other side of the pass, a posse was recruited from the Hole's settlers. The posse members included many of the valley's earliest and most well-known pioneers.[135]

Two alleged outlaws were gunned down and more than fifty missing horses bearing the "holy cross" brand – Chapman's brand – were recovered at Pierce Cunningham's Ranch in northern Jackson Hole, where the purported rustlers had over wintered.[136] Cunningham had settled at the site in 1886, and had innocently rented out his homestead to the alleged rustlers that winter. The shootout became known as the Cunningham Ranch Incident.[137]

The killing of the two alleged horse thieves at the Cunningham Ranch accomplished what the Montana regulators intended: it sent a strong and unmistakable message that ranchers were no longer going to tolerate rustling and horse thieves. It was a strong warning to anyone who may have had leanings toward engaging in the pre-owned livestock business, reinforcing the fears one survivor of the outlaw trail later expressed: "… no sleep, every time a piss ant rustled in the leaves, we thought a posse had caught up with us." It proved to be the last major outlaw event involving rustling in Jackson Hole.

On April 29, 1892, in the sensationalized journalism of the time, the *Cheyenne Daily Leader* proclaimed: "...special deputy J. H. Holland [was the leader] through the hazardous days...no man in Wyoming is a better man or citizen. He is the embodiment of law and order and is altogether one of such men as hew great and good commonwealths out of the wilderness." In closing, the editorial stated: "The impression that Jackson's Hole is peopled by rustlers and thieves is erroneous...their good name[s] should not be sullied in the public press by classing them with thieves, rustlers or regulators." You could say Cheyenne's newspaper's defensive sanctioning of frontier justice was a bit over blown.

Shortly afterward, Uinta County Commissioners appointed John Holland as Justice of the Peace and Robert Miller as Constable, giving the Cunningham Ranch affair some much needed legal whitewashing. [138] Holland, it was rumored, was a friend of one the more influential county commissioners.

After mulling over the Cunningham Ranch fracas, Jackson Hole's participants and settlers feared possible retribution from both the law and outlaws. They became reticent and vigilant, cloaking the episode in a "brotherhood" of secrecy and purposefully confounding details surrounding the incident. [139]

Decades later, Cal Carrington disclosed that when he first came into the valley in 1898, "... the 'brotherhood' was comprised of old timers who banded together to do what they wanted to do...they all went together... They all had a red squaw bandana for a badge... If you saw a man in the country riding around without a red bandana, you knew he was a stranger." [140]

John Holland's first case as Justice of the Peace came when hot-headed Dick Turpin had a felonious assault charge brought against him. Turpin had come up behind a settler named West and struck him forcefully on the head with his pistol. Turpin's justification was that West had trespassed and was mowing hay on what was Turpin's homestead ground. No doubt Turpin felt West was engaged in something akin to adverse possession or "claim jumping," a serious grievance in the West.

Carrington later recalled, "At the time of the trial there was no courthouse. It was held out on Holland's ranch… [in his] little ten-foot by twelve-foot log cabin. Turpin wasn't [found] guilty …and West [the plaintiff] was ordered out of the country. They all belonged to the brotherhood, so West had no chance; he went out."[141]

Years afterward, people attempting to look into or research early day proceedings discovered the Justice of Peace records for Jackson Hole had somehow disappeared or become lost.[142] If records were kept, their loss or disappearance contributes to an impression that those in office were safe-guarding themselves from any chance implication of wrong doing or outside repercussions.

Fredrick Remington's illustration of Bannock Indians hunting in Jackson Hole in the 1890s.
(Courtesy on-line file: Remington Bannock Indians Fording Snake)

12

JACKSON HOLE'S INDIAN WAR OF 1895

Nine Indians arrested, one killed, others escaped. Many Indians... here; threaten life and property. Settlers are moving families away. Want protection immediately. Action on your part is absolutely necessary. – July 18, 1895, telegram originating from Justice of the Peace Frank H. Rhodes and Constable William Manning, Marysvale (Jackson Hole), Wyoming, to Governor William A. Richards which resulted in the Secretary of War ordering the Ninth Calvary to Jackson Hole.

A chief source of subsistence and cash money in early-day Jackson Hole came from the valley's wildlife – predator bounties, hides, furs, meat, elk ivory (their eyeteeth were called "tusks"), and guiding sport hunters. Members of the Benevolent Order of Elks paid a premium for elk tusks, which were used to manufacture jewelry. Elk meat and hides could also be commercially sold for a premium in the 1890s. Jackson Hole resident's strong proprietary interest in the valley's wildlife grew not out of altruism or conservation, but from self-serving economic interest as competition for game and fur-bearers increased.

Market hunting for game meat was banned by Wyoming in 1895, but Idaho had no such laws. Commercial meat hunting was never a serious problem in Jackson Hole because of the distance and difficulty

Frontier cabin located along the Yellowstone River outside of Yellowstone National Park in Montana. Note the partially consumed game carcasses hanging on the side of the cabin and the person with a tamed elk calf. (Courtesy NPS, Yellowstone National Park On Line #03033)

of getting the meat to market. However, on the west slope of the Tetons and along the southwest corner of Yellowstone National Park, it was a different story. Hunters set up camps, dragging and horse-packing the carcasses in for skinning and butchering and smoking the meat. Then they hauled it by wagon to the distant railhead at St. Anthony. From there it was shipped and sold to hotels and construction companies in Salt Lake City.[143] It was a way to independently make some cash money, but it certainly was not easy money considering the great amount of labor and time that was involved.

While settlers elsewhere resolutely wiped out the bear, elk, and bighorn sheep, including the settlers and farmers across the mountains in Teton Basin, Idaho, at some point and on some level, many Jackson Hole residents recognized that a significant portion of their livelihood and subsistence was derived (and might continue to be in the future) from the area's plentiful wildlife.[144] Guide and outfitter businesses in Jackson Hole depended on the abundance of game animals, especially elk. [145]

The Wyoming Territorial Government implemented laws intended to protect game, particularly from commercial and year-round hunting, beginning as early as 1869. But killing wild animals was a profitable frontier endeavor.

The Territorial Legislature authorized bounties on wolves and mountain lions beginning in 1875. Continual bounty increases followed, so that by the twentieth century, killing large predatory animals had become a lucrative source of cash for experienced hunters and trappers.

The State and Grazing Association bounties, when combined, paid what was in those days, enormous sums of money for killing cougar and wolves – up to fifty dollars or more for a wolf. In addition, the wolf hide alone was worth seventy-five cents. Bear skins, claws, and skulls fetched twenty dollars and up; trophy heads of bighorn sheep, bison, and elk were each worth hundreds of dollars. The hides of elk also brought a premium and elk tusks were in big demand by the Benevolent and Protective Order of Elks for manufacture of jewelry. The elk tusks sold for five to twenty dollars a pair or more. There was a lot of monetary incentive for the killing of wild animals.

In 1899, each Wyoming resident was entitled by law to two deer, two elk, three antelope, and one mountain sheep. Earlier, bag limits were not a concern. Wyoming limits for non-residents were generous also, attracting out-of-state sportsmen. As late as 1905, for just fifty dollars, an out-of-state hunter was also entitled to two deer, two elk, and a bighorn sheep.

However, Jackson Hole's early inhabitants did not hunt by the calendar and there was little to no effective game law enforcement. Game appeared plentiful, so little or no attention was given to preventing wastefulness. Frontier attitudes prevailed: "game hogs," hide hunters, traders in trophies, and elk-tusk traffickers were a chronic problem and prevalent well into the twentieth century. Elk teeth were said to be the "coin of the realm" in early-day Jackson Hole. Game wardens were not too keen on looking for or bringing in game law offenders either, as it was a dangerous and poorly paid occupation.

Wildlife was a resource where the *Law of the Commons* applied; it was in an individual's self-interest to make maximum use of a resource held in common – "if you didn't, the other guy would." [146] One person's use, or a particular group of people's, use could preclude another's, even to the point of extinction of the resource. The destruction of the American bison in the nineteeth century is a classic example.[147] Some folks began to be concerned Jackson Hole's elk would suffer a similar fate as the bison.

Yellowstone Forest Reserve Superintendent A.A. Anderson learned the difficulty of enforcing the region's game laws firsthand. Around this time, Anderson met a young man on the trail with an out-of-season deer tied on his pack horse and arrested him. At the trial a six-man jury deliberated briefly and returned their verdict: "He did it, but we won't find him guilty this time."[148]

In a memoir, Charles W. Hedrick, stated the prevailing nineteenth century attitude regarding hunting: "There were game laws [back then], but it was the unwritten law that prospectors, trappers and the like [could] have what they wanted to eat in the way of wild game."[149]

Mary White, Jackson Hole's first post mistress located at Marysvale, recalled: "There was so much game wasted in those days…it makes me shudder to think of the times we have shot down a fat elk and taken only the hams and loins and left the rest for the coyotes."[150]

In September 1892, Theodore Roosevelt participated in an elk hunt in the vicinity of Two Ocean Pass in today's Teton Wilderness north of Jackson Hole. Roosevelt and the other hunter in his party, with the assistance of a guide, packer and wrangler, killed no less than ten or twelve bull elk and two bighorn sheep rams over the course of about two weeks. One of the bulls, Roosevelt claimed, was the largest he ever bagged. But still, he termed it "ill success," because for part of the trip they saw no elk at all.

Roosevelt attributed the absence of elk to "the presence of a great hunting-party of Shoshone Indians." In a published article, Roosevelt described the Native Americans' elk hunting methods that he observed: "Split into bands of eight or ten, they scoured the whole country on their tough, sure-footed ponies... and followed the elk wherever they went ... organizing great drives, the riders strung in lines far apart; they signaled to one another by willow whistles with which they also imitated the calling of bull elk ... they slew whatever they could ... but by preference cows and calves ... they were very persevering ... they not only wrought havoc among the elk, but also scared the survivors out of all the country over which they hunted."[151]

In the late nineteenth century, Jackson Hole's citizenry mostly practiced looking the other way when it came to game laws; but the neighborly practice, it turns out, was not extended to Native Americans. There a racially biased, double-standard was applied.

Settlers angrily resented Indians from the Fort Hall, Wind River, and Lemhi Agencies hunting in the valley and surrounding areas, even though Article 4 of the 1868 Fort Bridger Treaty assured them that right: "The Indians ... agree that they will make said reservation their permanent homes, and that they will make no permanent settlement elsewhere; but they shall have the right to hunt on the unoccupied land of the United States so long as the game may be found thereon, and so long as peace exists among the whites and Indians on the borders of the hunting districts."

The citizenry of Jackson Hole took uncompromising issue with the federal treaty rights, spreading exaggerated falsehoods bombastically peppered with hostile and racial slurs, claiming Native Americans were "wantonly and wastefully destroying game, threatening to deplete the region of big game, and destroying the livelihoods of professional guides in Jackson Hole."[152]

The issue came to a nasty head in 1894, when a "citizen committee" – a less-kind phrase would be vigilante committee – unanimously decided that Indians' hunting in Jackson Hole had to end. They collectively agreed that the State game laws should apply to Native Americans, too, and if the State was unable to enforce those laws, it would be done by a locally elected Constable and Justice of the Peace. Frank H. Rhodes was elected Justice, and William Manning was selected as Constable. Not too surprisingly each received forty votes, since both ran unopposed, representing nearly the entire valley populace at the time. [153]

Justice Rhodes contacted Wyoming Governor Richards and enlisted his support. Rhodes was assured by the Governor's office they would be protected in their actions. It was a collusive plan, one which has since been labeled "a conspiracy" by one historian, between the settlers of Jackson Hole and the state of Wyoming to dispossess the Native Americans of their treaty rights.

In hearings, Constable Manning later said: "We knew very well when we started on this thing that we would bring matters to a head. Someone was going to get killed, perhaps on both sides, and we decided that the sooner it was done the better, so that we could get the matter before the courts."[154]

The first incident in the summer of 1895 resulted in the arrest of three Indians in the Hoback drainage for violating game laws. They were brought before Justice Rhodes, who, without hesitation, imposed a fifteen dollar fine. The Indians didn't have any money, only some green elk hides, which had been confiscated. Settler John Carnes, to his credit, identified as "a squawman with a Bannock wife," was apparently a lone figure in disagreeing with the arrest; he voluntarily paid the fine so that the Indians would be released.[155]

A few weeks later, Constable Manning and his deputies took nine more Indians into custody within the Hoback area. They were also taken before Justice Rhoades, who once more imposed fines. And

Bannock Indians, n.d. (Courtesy of NPS, Yellowstone National Park On Line #02735)

again, the Indians had no money to pay their fines, so this time they were held under armed guard. After several days, the deputized settlers grew tired of guarding and feeding the prisoners. The Indians were given their horses back, and the guards claimed their captives "escaped."

Shortly thereafter, Manning and three deputies, again in the Hoback, confronted a larger Bannock hunting party, whose members were not willing to submit to arrest; one source says, "the redmen pulled their Winchesters."[156] Manning and his deputies sheepishly backed off and returned to Marysvale, complaining about how the Indians had disrespected the law.

The settlers felt they had to arrest those particular Indians, otherwise their cause would have become a laughingstock. Manning spent the next week recruiting twenty-six deputies from the local citizenry, the names of which are among Jackson Hole's most well-known early pioneers.[157] Carnes, Holland, and Miller, however, were not among them. (Carnes' wife was part Native American, and he may not have agreed with the posse's intentions; Holland appears to have been out of the valley, likely in Teton Basin, at his Horseshoe Creek Ranch; and Miller must have had other business to attend to besides riding with a posse.)

The posse's planned strategy was to travel up Cache Creek, circling back into Hoback Canyon from the east in order to gain the advantage of surprise. (Historian Jermy Wight points out that this was similar to General Custer's strategy undertaken at the Little Bighorn, "so the Indians wouldn't get away.")

At daylight, Manning and his deputized force located and surrounded an Indian camp, taking all of them prisoner. They put up no resistance. However, it turned out *not* to be the group of Indians who had resisted

arrest earlier. Instead, this encampment consisted of nine Bannock men
and thirteen women with five children.

At the mouth of Granite Creek in Hoback Canyon, at the place called
Battle Mountain today, Manning began to fear his captives were
going to try to run for it. He gave an order for the posse members
to load their weapons and chamber a round, telling them that if the
Indians tried to escape to shoot their horses.

When the clattering of gun mechanisms sounded, the Indians
scattered, fearing they were all about to be massacred. In the melee
that followed, an unarmed elderly and nearly blind Indian was shot
in the back and killed; a twenty-year old Indian youth was shot twice
but escaped even though wounded; a six-month old infant was lost
from his fleeing mother's arms and never found; and a little boy,
along with the Native Americans' horses, were taken into custody.

Re-gathering the next morning, the frightened Bannocks avoided
the posse and peacefully made their way back to the Fort Hall
Reservation. Constable Manning and his twenty-six deputies rode
triumphantly back to Marysvale with their prisoner – a terrified
four-year-old Indian boy. It was the last of Manning's Indian hunting
sorties.

Fearing retaliation from the Indians, Jackson Hole settlers panicked.
They forted-up at several locations: Spread Creek, Marysvale, Wilson,
and possibly Robert Miller's place, everyone armed with a rifle. A
correspondent wrote, the settler's at the Wilson fortification were
"huddled together in [Nick] Wilson's log cabin…one vigorous and
massive lady is especially fierce in her denunciation of the troop's slow
movement…she is skeptical they will kill any Indians when they get
there, calling the Indians 'government pets.'"[158]

Justice Rhodes and Constable Manning wired Governor Richards that immediate protection was required for Jackson Hole, that a large number of Indians were threatening immediate attack. A call for federal troops to intervene followed from the Governor. Exaggerated rumors were rampant. Wyoming officials publicly denounced the "bloodthirsty redskins." The nearest telegraph was at Market Lake, Idaho (a railroad siding, the name was later changed to Roberts), which frantically clicked and clattered sending hyperbolized and garbled bits and pieces of misinformation across the wires, like in the child's game of "pass it along."[159]

The reports and news became grossly distorted and sensationalized. *The New York Times*, the *Baltimore Morning Herald*, and the *Cheyenne Tribune* newspapers reported shocking news in bold, front-page July 27, 1895 headlines:

"An Awful Massacre Occurred at Jackson's Hole,
Every Settler Was Killed,
Butchered by Red Devils
– Troops are too Late –
Men, Women and Children Killed
– NOT ONE ESCAPED."

"BUTCHERD BY BANNOCKS
– AN AWFUL MASSACRE AT JACKSON'S HOLE –
TROOPS ARRIVE TOO LATE. "

The initial report of the massacre was received at the Union Pacific headquarters in Omaha, Nebraska, from Market Lake. The telegraph agent at Market Lake declared the information "perfectly reliable."

On July 19, settler Robert Miller, avowed by the State's Auditor to be a "very intelligent and reliable gentleman," petitioned the Wyoming Governor's Office by letter to have federal troops sent to Jackson

Settlers forted up at Camp Wilson in Wilson, Wyoming, during Jackson Hole's 1895 Indian War.
(Courtesy of John J. Coppinger Collection, American Heritage Center, University of Wyoming, Laramie)

Hole. Miller wrote: "We are banded here at my place, having fortified ourselves to make a desperate fight…It is haying time, and here we are compelled to protect ourselves, allowing our homes and stock to be at the mercy of the Indians."[160]

Meanwhile, adjacent Fremont County, Wyoming, got caught up in the hullabaloo, too. There were whisperings that "armed Indians and signal fires" were seen northwest of Lander, around Oregon Buttes, by a miner. A large public gathering was held in Lander, where it was proposed to "send a body of one hundred citizens strong to assist the settlers of Jackson Hole." The *Sun-Leader*, Lander's newspaper, reported Sheriff Grimmett and Ex-Sheriff Sparhawk of Fremont County were "hand picking fifty men mounted on horses selected for endurance … using great care in arming the men so as to do good service should they chance to meet the foe." They planned to place a detachment in each of the passes leading into Jackson Hole, "and give the redskins a warm reception should they come that way."[161]

General John J. Coppinger deployed with the Ninth Cavalry from Fort Robinson, Nebraska, on July 25. The Ninth Cavalry was a segregated African-American regiment, known as the "Buffalo Soldiers." A cheering ovation marked their passage through Cheyenne. Less than three days later, in a rapid deployment by railroad, the Ninth Calvary and a sixty-two mule pack train had arrived at Market Lake, Idaho.

The day before, on July 27, Jackson Hole resident Will Simpson had written the Governor's Office in Cheyenne that volunteers from among the settlers were "scouring the country everyday looking for Indian camps…[and] we are looking for troops at once…the soldiers will at least bring relief to the settlers, so they can make hay. Failure to make hay means that every settler will be poverty stricken."[162]

The Ninth Calvary fording the Snake River near Wilson, Wyoming, in 1895.
(Courtesy of John J. Coppinger Collection, American Heritage Center, University of Wyoming, Laramie)

The soldiers laid over a day for the horses and mules to recover from riding in the railroad's stable cars; then, following two days hard marching, they bivouacked in Teton Basin near Moose Creek at the base of Teton Pass. The next day the troops crossed Teton Pass. In 1889, the Wilson-Cheney families, who settled at the base of the pass, and for whom the town of Wilson is named, had spent two weeks hauling six wagons over Teton Pass. Six years later, the Ninth Calvary accomplished the considerable feat of moving all their wagons, horses, pack train, and equipment across and into Wilson in one long day.

But then the soldiers required the next two days fording the Snake River's powerful currents. Reportedly, one wagon over turned and a team was lost in the swift water. By August 3rd, the cavalry had a field camp set up along Flat Creek near Marysvale and immediately sent out two reconnaissance patrols. No Indians were to be found anywhere.

Lander's sheriff's posse also reported that they had "ridden fully 400 miles and the only Indians they had seen were on the Shoshone Reservation." However, Lander's Ex- Sheriff Sparhawk, who had led a posse, but who officially no longer held the sheriff's position, publicly expressed the opinion that "the Indians were waiting to attack until after the soldiers leave Jackson Hole."[163]

A related incident took place when "six tinhorns" from the Lander posse, in passing through the valley, burglarized the unoccupied cabins of settlers Arnn and Holland, removing bedding and clothing. Will Simpson and Arnn (the same Bill Arnn who was living in Jackson Hole in the winter of 1884-85 among Teton Jackson's gang and Carnes, Holland and Miller) tracked the itinerate riff-raff from Lander for thirty miles before catching up with them. According to Simpson's account, Arnn proved to be a cool hand. In a standoff with the nefarious bunch, Simpson says he was "scared to death," but

Arnn drew his revolver and warned: "The first S.O.B. that tries to pull his gun, I'm going to kill," which prevented a gunfight and allowed recovery of the stolen goods.[164]

In fact, historian Betts notes, "… during the Bannock War, the only pillaging that had been done [was]…done by white men." All the while the Indians had been in the valley, not a single theft was reported.[165]

The Ninth Calvary spent a month in Jackson Hole. They "encamped in a beautiful spot," and were said to have "enjoyed life there," while varying their Army rations with a diet of fish and various game. The stay provided a nice break for them from barracks life in Nebraska. They reportedly "played 'mouth harps' and sang." The African-American troops were a great curiosity to the valley residents.[166]

General Coppinger and a special cavalry work party left Jackson Hole to return east by the way of Togwotee Pass. The general's work crew improved the Togwotee Pass trail into a passable wagon road on their way out.

Investigations that followed declared the whole affair a "premeditated and prearranged plan" to kill some Indians, stir up some trouble, and get the Native Americans shut out of Jackson Hole. One report labeled it, "atrocious, cold-blooded murder for a mere game law violation." But investigators unanimously agreed: it would be useless to try to bring the men to trial considering the predominant anti-Indian sentiment in the Jackson Hole community and throughout the state. No jury in Uinta County, Wyoming, would have found them guilty.[167]

A second legal issue was the validity of the Fort Bridger Treaty of 1868, allowing the Indians to hunt on unoccupied public lands. The Federal Circuit Court in Cheyenne found that the State game laws were in conflict with the federal treaty, and therefore were not enforceable. As if preplanned, and it may well have been, the finding was immediately appealed to the United States Supreme Court. In May 1896, the Supreme Court, in a vote of five to one, reversed the Circuit Court determination and issued a landmark decision saying, "it was within the State's right to establish and enforce game laws."

The case ended up back in Cheyenne with a District Court judge admonishing the Indians for illegal hunting in Wyoming in a test case involving an arrested Bannock tribesman who had volunteered to serve as a surrogate. The settlers of Jackson Hole had prevailed, accomplishing what they set out to do – put an end to Native American hunting in Jackson Hole.[168]

Afterward, Wyoming Governor Richards took it a step further, announcing that the Lemhi and Ute Indians were *not* part of the Fort Bridger Treaty and had absolutely no right to hunt buffalo on Wyoming's Red Desert: "If they undertake to do so they will be arrested … if they resist arrest they do it at their own peril." The warning was further stated to include all Indians, as "…few if any officers of this state can tell a Bannock from a Ute, or a Shoshone from a Lemhi, even at close range."[169]

It is not generally known that buffalo still existed on the Red Desert, the vast public domain lands in south-central Wyoming, as late as 1895. At that time, few wild bison were left alive anywhere. Not wanting to attract national attention, Wyoming State officials were disinclined to make it publicly known. Yellowstone Park had less than a hundred bison remaining by then and poachers were rapidly decimating those; by 1902, only twenty-five bison still survived in Yellowstone. While Governor Richards was vocal in declaring the bison off-limits to the Indians, Wyoming never afforded them protection from white hunters. Today, bison no longer exist on the Red Desert.[170]

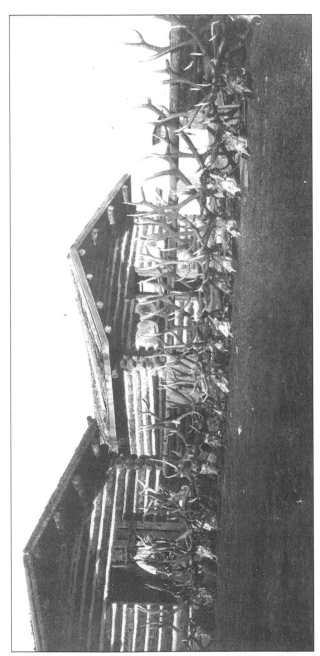

A line up of a single season's trophy elk heads taken by the hunting clients of an early day Jackson Hole guide and outfitter.
(Courtesy of Jackson Hole Historical Society and Museum 1985.1016.001p)

13
OTHER MOUNTAIN LAW EPISODES

The Elk Tusk Poachers

"Until my present [inspection] trip…I had no idea of the number of the number of elk being slaughtered…a large portion merely for their tusks. In a small grove near where I camped last night I counted the bodies of ten elk…killed last winter; no portion of the carcasses had been touched except [for] the removal of the tusks." – Forest Reserve Superintendent A.A. Anderson in a 1901 letter to President Theodore Roosevelt.

In 1897, only two years after the settlers and Wyoming officials dispossessed Native Americans of their hunting rights in Jackson Hole, allegedly because the Indians were "wantonly and wastefully killing elk," complaints were filed with the Secretary of Interior by Colonel S.B.M. Young, Acting Superintendent of Yellowstone National Park, citing an ongoing slaughter of elk in Jackson Hole. The illegal carnage was being carried out by whites, not the Indians, who believed they had a God-given right to exploit to exhaustion any and all natural resources available to them. Frontier attitudes still prevailed in the valley.[171]

Colonel Young noted state protection of wildlife was a failure and recommended extending military authority into Jackson Hole to control the serious poaching problem. Teton Forest Reserve

Superintendent A.A. Anderson reached the same conclusions.[172]
Likewise, in 1895, General Coppinger's report had also suggested
extending the Yellowstone National Park boundary south to include
Jackson Hole to resolve the "uncontrolled hunting and fishing
there."[173]

In 1899, Wyoming officials finally appointed a single game warden,
Jackson Hole settler Albert T. Nelson, whose impossible job it was to
enforce hunting laws across the entire state – "the lone guardian of
the entire State's wildlife."[174]

Born in Sweden, Nelson immigrated to the United States at a young
age in 1883, where he worked on ranches in Nebraska, coal mines at
Rock Springs and the gold mines at South Pass, Wyoming, He drifted
into Jackson Hole in 1895 to prospect for gold, and in 1897, took up
a homestead along the Gros Ventre River above Kelly.[175]

Nelson became a man of many self-taught talents. He practiced
taxidermy and photography, was a devoted gardener, an excellent
builder, rancher, and a renown hunting guide. Reportedly among his
clients over the years were the Harrimans, J. D. Rockefeller, Ernst
Thompson Seton, and painter Carl Rungius. But as warden, Nelson
discovered enforcing the game laws was discouragingly impossible.

He was required to travel to Evanston and Cheyenne on his $100
a month salary for jury trials on any arrests he might make and
obtaining a conviction was next to impossible. Moreover, the
notorious poachers and hardened criminals, whose job it was for him
to control, were literally his next door neighbors in Kelly. Nelson
resigned after three years of his four-year term.[176]

Game wardens that lived and worked in the local community had
their hands full and a tightrope to walk. The elk-teeth traffickers,

called "tuskers," blatantly ignored the law which allowed residents two elk per person a year.

Elk teeth were small and easy to transport and they had a ready market. Poachers killed elk whenever the chance availed, simply for the value of their teeth, which was five to ten dollars a pair or more. At a time when wages were only thirty dollars a month, if any job was to be had, that was plenty of monetary incentive for killing elk.[177] Game wardens were not overly aggressive in pursuing and arresting game law offenders. It was dangerous, poorly-paid work, and it made for very unsettled relationships with one's neighbors.[178]

Dealers in elk ivory went so far as to advertise in local papers. Settler Will Simpson even reported observing tusks being sold in the presence of a local deputy game warden. Game protection in Jackson Hole was denounced by outsiders as "a farce." Accusations of incompetence were leveled against the Hole's forest rangers, game wardens, and the justice of the peace, seemingly to little or no avail.[179] In 1902, *Outdoor Life* published a series of letters pointing out the ineffective wildlife protection in Wyoming, particularly Jackson Hole.[180]

When photographer Frederic Irland, Frank Petersen's client, visited Jackson Hole in the spring of 1903 for the purposes of photographing elk, he wrote an article for *Scribner's Magazine*. In it he said, "Everybody in that part of the country talked about elk, in the same way that Glouchester people talk about codfish…" And, while "It was against the law to sell elk tusks … almost everyman I met privately exhibited to me at least one pair."[181]

One renowned elk tusker who operated in the Yellowstone and Jackson Hole area was a settler named William Binkley. Originally from Kansas, in 1901, he settled near the town of Kelly along the

Convicted Jackson Hole elk tuskers and Yellowstone National Park game poachers, William Binkley (left) and Charles Purdy, awaiting incarceration at the Fort Yellowstone Guardhouse in Yellowstone National Park. Binkley, who homesteaded in Jackson Hole, was a hard case who had previously spent time in the Idaho Penitentiary for horse rustling.

(Courtesy of the Ken and Lenore Diem Collection, Box 42, American Heritage Center, University of Wyoming, Laramie, Wyoming)

Gros Ventre River with his wife and four children. As frontiersmen were wont to do, he made a living through a variety of means – proved up on a homestead, ran a few head of cattle, raised a garden, guided sport hunters, and worked as a butcher and a teamster.

However, Binkley couldn't resist the opportunity to make some additional cash money. He became a hardened poacher, a notorious tusker, and a local broker of animal parts; illegally managing the buying, selling, and transport of hides, elk horns, and particularly, elk tusks, for others, as well as himself. He bragged he was an "ivory merchant."[182]

Binkley had a criminal record before coming to Jackson Hole. In 1893, he had been convicted of grand larceny for rustling cattle and horses in Kootenai and Latah counties, Idaho, and sentenced to a year in the Idaho Penitentiary.[183]

Binkley, it was said, did his killing with a small caliber rifle, so the sound of the shot could not be heard from far way, preferably just before a snow storm to cover the evidence. After killing an elk, he wouldn't approach it for several days, leaving no trace and guarding against the unlikely chance that a game warden might investigate the shot.

Brinkley and some others teamed up to make some serious money from poaching and illegal trafficking of game heads, elk teeth, and hides; they became known as the "Binkley-Purdy-Isabel gang."[184] At the time, Purdy was a trapper who lived on Fish Creek and Isabel a bounty hunter for cougar and wolves.[185]

For years, they and other poachers pretty much enjoyed *carte blanche* in the Jackson Hole area. Not that the authorities – state game wardens, U.S. Forest Service and National Park personnel, and the

Department of Justice – weren't fully engaged in trying to apprehend what one warden termed "the lawless vagabonds," they were. In fact, the prolonged and frustrating attempts to put Binkley, Purdy, and Isabel behind bars became one of the most publicized criminal cases ever in Jackson Hole.[186] One official later wrote: "The truth of the matter was that they were afraid of Binkley... the [wardens] down in Jackson Hole didn't dare arrest him."[187]

Jackson Hole settlers were still worried about possible repercussions from the Cunningham Ranch incident, but they nevertheless persisted with the practice of vigilante actions – Mountain Law as it was known. They stubbornly held fast to the belief that they, not the authorities in Evanston, were best suited to deal with local problems. The valley was still was an isolated outpost where the local citizenry, if and when people got fed up, policed themselves.

Years passed, poaching mostly continued unchecked, but around 1906, a group of twenty settlers, allegedly led by Otho Williams, a surveyor who settled in the valley in 1900, decided that enough was enough. They formed a vigilance committee comprised of individuals who were said to be "willing to hold the end of a rope."

Hanging the tuskers, considered as an option, was voted down. Instead, three of the toughest members from the group were elected to confront Binkley and his gang and deliver an ultimatum: "Clear out within forty-eight hours or be shot." The ominous warning was delivered at night, perhaps by masked riders. Binkley and Purdy wisely heeded the notice, packing up and leaving Jackson Hole by way of Teton Pass a few days later.[188] Two days after that, Jackson Hole game wardens reported Mrs. Binkley and her children followed, crossing Teton Pass with two wagons loaded with "elk heads, antlers, and household items."[189]

Many Jackson Hole histories give the impression that the poaching problem ended when Binkley and Purdy cleared town after the Mountain Law ultimatum, but it was not that simple. The two poachers first went only as far as the saloons in Driggs and St. Anthony, Idaho. Still tending to their grisly business, on the first of November, they sent a freight shipment from St. Anthony comprised of eighty-three pairs of elk antlers, many still attached to skulls, elk scalps, bear hides, and other items via the Oregon Short Line Railroad to a taxidermist in Los Angles, California.[190]

A few days later, Binkley and Purdy followed, but they were met and arrested at the Los Angeles freight depot by a California game warden and a United States Marshal, and their shipment seized. They were charged with and plead guilty to "interstate commerce of game killed in violation of local laws" and were fined $200. After which they were immediately rearrested and charged with killing elk within Yellowstone National Park – a felony. The hearings and legal wrangling for the two men went on over a period of three years, during which time the two men were held in the Idaho Penitentiary in Boise and the Bannock County Jail in Pocatello, Idaho. Finally they were sentenced to the Fort Yellowstone Guardhouse.[191]

Within little more than a month of confinement there, Binkley escaped, "disappeared into thin air," and was never seen again. While many rumors circulated regarding his whereabouts, most believe he eventually made his way into Mexico. Mrs. Binkley, after a period of time, also vanished. Isabel, likewise skedaddled and was seen no more after he was also indicted for killing elk in Yellowstone National Park.[192]

Charles Purdy, on the other hand, after serving out his jail sentences, built himself a cabin residence at Loon Lake, Idaho, an isolated spot next to the southwest corner of Yellowstone National Park. Purdy had a deeply ingrained frontier attitude that people should be able to live their lives however they wished, "without interference" from the law or government.[193] He became a locally admired outdoorsman, one who it was said, "could survive in the wilderness." In winter, using twelve-foot, home-made skis, he would travel from his cabin across the Conant Trail to Moran, Wyoming.

Purdy also expanded his illicit repertoire to include operating hidden stills along Yellowstone Park's border and bootlegging moonshine. When he died in 1936, his death certificate listed his occupation as "prospector and trapper." Purdy is buried in Mountainview Cemetery at Pocatello, Idaho. Purdy Basin in the Gros Ventre Mountains is named after him.

The practice of elk-tusk hunting in the Jackson Hole region came to a close only after demand and prices declined.[194]

The Sheep Wars

SHEEPMEN WARNING
We will not permit sheep to graze upon the elk ranges in Jackson Hole. Govern yourselves accordingly. Signed: The Settlers of Jackson Hole. – Sign posted on Teton Pass as recalled by settler Stephen N. Leek in *A Place Called Jackson Hole.*

Domestic sheep were never welcome on public lands in Jackson Hole. Grazing sheep can nibble plants down to their root crowns, and their sharp hooves cut into the soil and destroy plant root systems. Improperly managed sheep grazing can adversely impact range productivity. Cattlemen viewed sheep as "destroyers of open range." For a period of time, signs were posted on Teton Pass and other approaches to the valley warning herders away from entering Jackson Hole. The valley's livestock industry was ruled by cattlemen who passionately detested sheep. Sheep were disliked second only to horse thieves and cattle rustlers. Jackson Hole cowboy and hunting guide Enoch Cal Carrington pretty much summed up the cattle rancher's attitude when he expressed his distaste for sheep: "I had no use for sheep…wouldn't even wear woolen socks or such trash as that."[195]

Jackson Hole cattlemen kept a watchful eye that sheep grazing did not spill over the mountains from Idaho or Utah and cross their imaginary boundary into the valley. However, it wasn't only the potential competition with cattle grazing they took exception to, Jackson Hole's citizenry also fretted sheep grazing would detrimentally impact the valley's elk ranges.

In 1896, sheep men attempted to take their woolly critters into Jackson Hole. They were turned back and driven out by "grim-faced, guns in hand" Jackson Hole ranchers before they could cross the Snake River into the main part of the valley.[196]

In August 1901, violence broke out after a herder crossed into the Hole along Mosquito Creek near Teton Pass. A vigilance committee took it upon themselves to resolve the sheep problem once and for all. Historian B.W. Driggs, *History of Teton Valley,* records that a sheep herder from Rexburg, Idaho, crossed over the mountain divide onto the Jackson side. Stockmen from Jackson Hole, wearing masks, claimed "the sheep were encroaching on the elk range and began exterminating them. The firing and stampeding resulted in the death of about 300 animals…they killed the owner's horse and dog, burned the camp equipment… [the sheep owner] begged for his life, promising the raiders he would leave."

The names of the Jackson Hole settlers who participated in this affair were never spoken in more than guarded whispers and have been lost to time. Those in the sheep industry heeded the warning, however.

Like the Native Americans six years earlier, they were effectively shut
out of using public lands in Jackson Hole.

The frontier belief that elk were and always would be plentiful began
to be questioned after the severe winter of 1908-1909. By then,
settlement had begun to encroach heavily on game habitat, cutting
the animals off from their historic winter ranges and migration
routes. Elk died by the thousands that winter. Jackson Hole residents
were shocked; a decade earlier game and other natural resources had
seemed limitless.

Early settlers Robert Miller and Stephen Leek found themselves
in the conservationist's camp, contributing meaningfully to the
establishment of a National Elk Refuge: Leek took photographs,
toured and, lectured in its support, while Miller sold his 1,760-
acre ranch to the federal government, which served as the core
property for the new refuge. The Issac Walton League assisted as well,
purchasing another thirty-five homesteads for the refuge. Miller,
Leek, and other settlers, had witnessed great changes in Jackson Hole
and the community's attitudes, compared to those of early years.

The town of Jackson in 1907. A canvas covered wagon box at Marysvale served as Jackson Hole's first post office for several years in the early 1890s, until the post office was moved to Maggie Simpson's homestead on Cache Creek. She named it Jackson.

(Courtesy of Jackson Hole Historical Society and Museum 1958.0225.001p)

14
DEVELOPED HOMESTEADS BECOME A COMMODITY

About twelve years ago, the first settlement was made in Jackson's Hole, the first settlers being engaged in stock raising. It underwent the usual experience of a frontier settlement. Some disreputable characters came in there and the place was given a bad name. Later, a better class of citizens came in, post offices were established, farms opened, and the disreputable class was driven out. – Wyoming Governor, William A. Richards, July 30, 1895.

Contrary to the Governor's remarks above, the "disreputable characters" were not all "driven out" of Jackson Hole by 1895. It was another decade and more before that became a *fait accompli* – an accomplished fact that could not be undone.

As the frontier gave way to settlement and civilization, some that had known the classless society and freedom of the Old West began searching for what had been lost. To their chagrin, they discovered the frontier was no more. The vast wild herds, wilderness and open spaces, large predators, the Indians, the best homestead ground, and a way of life, had all slipped away within what was a relatively short time. Pundits had predicted it would take centuries to settle the West; instead it was only decades.

Already, in 1892, William Hubbard, an early settler in Teton Valley, had decided: "This country is getting too damn thick with Mormon [settlers] ... [my brother] Frank is getting sick of staying here. The winters are too damn long. It is too much work to take care of stock."[197]

Feeling crowded by more arrivals was not an uncommon frontier sentiment. Historian John Daugherty recorded that in the 1890s, a Jackson Hole settler referred to as "old man Atherton," became upset when a dozen folks showed up for a Fourth of July picnic at Jenny Lake. Disgusted, he swore "people were getting too darn numerous." Atherton abandoned his cabin on Flat Creek in Jackson Hole and moved to a more isolated location up the GrosVentre River. Atherton Creek, a tributary of the Gros Ventre River, is named after him. Today, we can hardly imagine living within the incredibly deep solitude the earliest inhabitants of the Hole experienced or like that which Atherton preferred and sought out.

Another frontiersman, Thomas E. Crawford, was put off by the changes, too. He remarked in his published *Recollections*: "I made my last trip into Jackson Hole during 1900 ... [it] was filled up with pilgrims and didn't look good to me anymore."[198]

In 1899, Charles "Pop" Delony opened the first mercantile store in the valley. It was located on the Simpson Ranch. Delony provided an "amazing variety" of goods for sale: glass, door and window frames, lumber, nails, hardware, dry goods – all the items, which before, settlers had to obtain from outside sources and freight long distances into the valley. Even still, winter and the spring flood waters continued to cut off supplies.[199]

The 1900 census revealed 638 people residing in Jackson Hole. Over the next nine years, as homesteaders continued to pour in, the

Hole's population swelled to 1,500 residents. Those numbers reflect an astounding increase of twenty-five times more people over the 1890 census estimate of just sixty. By the beginning of the twentieth century, sixty-five homesteads existed immediately north of the town site of Jackson alone, on what is today the National Elk Refuge.[200] The town site of Jackson was platted in 1901.[201]

In 1901, in a move further civilizing the surrounding valley, an Army unit from Yellowstone National Park and Forest Reserve inspector I.A. Marcum investigated and cited fourteen "trespassers on the Forest Reserve ... recommending removal of all individuals having no legal right of residence. " The illegal squatters were found to be making a living from the Forest Reserves, "largely from game." The action was a step in the difficult task of distinguishing between legitimate settlers and unlawful squatters, and removing the latter. Marcum concluded his report, saying: "From what I saw and heard while there, I think this is the most lawless place I have [ever] seen."[202]

Histories generally state Carnes and Holland sold their homesteads to David and Ben Goe and left Jackson Hole before 1900, "disappearing from the pages of local history," which was only partly true. [203] There is more to their story than just the common frontier practice of "moving on." Proving up and selling their homesteads was not so simple, at least not for John Holland.

Carnes and Holland did not actually prove up on their homestead claims until March 1896 and January 1897, respectively.[204] That is twelve or thirteen years after the traditionally given date of their Jackson Hole settlement, and more if one accepts that they were there before 1884. The necessary land survey allowing them to secure title was not completed until 1893.

Historian Fern Nelson explained the delay by noting, "Sometimes

patents were held up in the land office for quite some time." Others
believe Holland had actually left Jackson Hole by 1890, after selling
a "relinquishment right" to his homestead.[205] Turns out that neither
government delay nor relinquishment were the sole reasons. Also, like
many, Carnes and Holland probably had a dislike for completing the
necessary bureaucratic paperwork, too.

They were not alone. Bachelor settler John Cherry took a record
nineteen years to prove up on a Desert Land Entry in the Buffalo
Valley in the northern-part of Jackson Hole. Cherry's claim was
complicated by his having to overcome the government declaring it
"fraudulent." [206]

Carnes and Holland both seem to have realized somewhat late
in the game that having title to their respective homesteads was
necessary to fully capitalize on the influx of new settlers. At the close
of the nineteenth century, many of those were seeking to purchase
developed homesteads. It was a virtual land boom for the time. You
could say it was the beginning of the demand for one of the valley's
most valued commodities, one which continues strongly today – real
estate.

Those who chose not to sell, such as Moses Giltner, Robert Miller,
Frank Petersen, and Jack Shive, became life-long residents, cherished
by Jackson Hole's citizenry, in later years, for being some of the
valley's original pioneers and "old timers."

Copy of John Carnes' original Homestead Patent .
(Courtesy Jackson Hole Historical Society and Museum)

15
MOVING ON – SETTLING ISN'T NECESSARILY PERMANENT

Watch the procession of civilization, marching single file – the buffalo…
the Indian, the fur trader and hunter, the cattle raiser, the pioneer farmer
– and the frontier has passed by. – Fredrick Jackson Turner

The Carnes Move to Fort Hall
In 1895, two years before he obtained patent for his Jackson Hole
homestead, grazing association records show John Carnes was
running fifty-one head of cattle. He received his homestead patent
in 1897, signed by President Grover Cleveland.[207] Three years later,
in January 1900, he sold and transferred the title of his homestead to
Charles Allen, from the Budge-Allen party who temporarily used his
and Holland's cabins in 1896.

In 1910, Allen sold Carnes' original homestead to David Goe, who
two years later transferred the property to his brother, Ben Goe.[208] Ben
Goe was the person who later started the Cowboy Bar in Jackson. After
the sale of their homestead, John and Millie moved to the Shoshone-
Bannock Reservation at Fort Hall, Idaho. Their original Jackson Hole
homestead eventually became part of the National Elk Refuge.

Rumors of involvement with horse thievery followed Carnes to Fort

Hall. As Cal Carrington remembered it, Ed Harrington's mother ran a rooming house in Denver. After Harrington was released from jail sometime in the early twentieth century, he worked in Denver at the race track. Harrington and an accomplice allegedly used the opportunity to steal four fillies and a valuable stud from the track's pasture.

According to Carrington, Carnes purportedly arranged for the stolen horses to be wintered on the Fort Hall Indian Reservation, where they wouldn't be found. The following spring, the horses were taken on to Jackson Hole, where the stallion was used for breeding. "Afterwards they shot him… couldn't keep him, y'know, someone would have come along and noticed him right away."[209]

Millie Sorelle passed away in 1923 at Fort Hall, when Carnes was eighty-four years old. He was sent to the Old Soldiers' Home at Boise. The confinement was too much for the old frontiersman, though, and they couldn't get him to stay there. He kept running away, incredibly, somehow finding his way 260-miles back to Fort Hall. Carnes spent his last years with Harry Hutchinson, a friend at Fort Hall. He died in 1931 at age ninety-two.[210]

Carnes' obituary states: "He was the first white man to farm in Jackson Hole and took the farm machinery into that place piece by piece on pack horses when there were not even trails to follow. At one time he was deputy sheriff and as such was sent to disperse a band of horse and cattle thieves that infested the region. As he always expressed it, 'We were sent in after them, and they are there yet.'"[211] John was undoubtedly referring to the Cunningham Ranch incident. The alleged rustlers were buried nearby in a shallow grave. It is rumored that for years afterward, the graves kept washing out, exposing their bones.

John Holland Proves Up and
Sells His Jackson Hole Homestead

The story of John Holland's Jackson Hole homestead title and transfer is not as tidy and neat as Carnes'. Holland's homestead case file in the National Archives shows he paid $300 to obtain a "Pre-Emption Proof" in April 1894, which had an expiration date of September 1896.

Curiously, Holland filed the proof in Fremont County at Lander, Wyoming, instead of Uinta County at Evanston, Wyoming. A May 14, 1894, document "Number 35" also shows a payment of $199.20 was made entitling John H. Holland to receive Patent.

Additionally, a Wyoming Government Land Office record documents a cash homestead entry on March 26, 1896.[212] Both of those patent documents, however, appear to be missing. If they were issued, they seem to either have become lost or were never recorded.

There's more to figure out in Holland's land dealings. Teton County, Wyoming, records show Holland had already deeded the same homestead to Maud Carpenter for $500 in June 1894.[213] Maud in turn sold this property to George Campbell on July 15, 1896 for $500. David Goe obtained the property from Campbell's estate in 1906 and transferred it to Ben Goe six years later.[214]

Holland's 1894 deed to Maud was prepared and executed in Fremont County, Idaho (it was before Teton County, Idaho, existed). Maud's deed to Campbell was prepared in Driggs, Idaho, also, and was signed in the presence of Teton Basin store owner and local civic leader Don C. Driggs.[215] Holland's original homestead ground, like that of John Carnes', was eventually acquired by the federal government to become part of the National Elk Refuge.

Holland's 1894 Pre-Emption Proof testimony contains some

interesting asides. His post office address was given as Marysvale, Wyoming (Fred White's homestead, the town of Jackson did not exist yet at that time).[216] Neighbors Robert E. Miller, John R. Carnes, William T. Crawford, and John Hicks, all of Marysvale, were named as witnesses.[217]

Carnes and Miller both testified that Holland's improvements consisted of "a seventeen by seventeen foot" log house, a fourteen by two-hundred foot log stable, corrals, one-mile of fencing, and one-and-one-half miles irrigating ditches," all of which was valued at $750. Holland further stated he cultivated about "fifteen acres of small grain and vegetables [and] fifty acres to hay." Carnes swore that he had known Holland for seventeen years, since 1877. Miller claimed he knew him for eight years, exactly matching Holland's sworn 1886 settlement date.[218]

Holland testified he "first made settlement" on the land in July 1886 and that his first act of settlement was "building a house." He further states that he did not establish actual residence on the land until June 1887; and that after 1887, his residence there was continuous.[219] Both Carnes and Miller corroborated those statements.[220]

Readers may recognize discrepancies between Holland's testimony above and his 1883 water right filing, the 1885 statements of Simpson and Arnn, and other records mentioned earlier. Why did Holland appear to provide false dates on his proof application? Moreover, his neighbors, Carnes and Miller, substantiated those dates, which appear to be bogus.

Maybe Holland and the others simply didn't recall the years accurately. On the other hand, perhaps he was aware of, or may have been involved in, some shady doings prior to 1886 and did not want to testify that he was residing in Jackson Hole during that time period. While it can not be proven, the confounding of dates may have been purposeful as it avoided the possibility of self-incrimination.

The Hollands Move to Teton Basin

While ambiguous in other historical accounts, it is true that John Holland did leave Jackson Hole sometime in the 1890s, around the time when he was trying to gain title to his Jackson Hole homestead and then sell it.

During those years, he was going back and forth from Jackson Hole to Teton Basin, Idaho, where he met and courted Maud Carpenter, the daughter of Dan "Dad" Carpenter, a Civil War veteran living in the Basin. The fact that Holland was not among Manning's posse members in 1895, further suggests he was outside of the area at the time.

When Cal Carrington first arrived in Teton Basin in April 1897, he filed for a water right on the "surplus water from John Holland's spring."[221] This was when Holland and Carrington first met. Years later, Carrington recalled that "when Holland went out to Idaho [over Teton Pass from Jackson Hole] to get provisions, he got acquainted with Dan "Dad" Carpenter's youngest daughter [Maud]. Carpenter was an old Civil War vet living on the Teton River at the time. Holland married her and then moved over to Teton Basin. There was where I got acquainted with him."[222]

Maud Carpenter was born in Iowa. Both her parents were originally from New York.[223] She claimed she and Holland were married on the 4th of July, 1894, when she was 21 years old. [224] He was twenty years older. Their first son, Edwin John, was born May 9, 1895.[225] Curiously, though, they had used her maiden name, Carpenter, in the real estate transaction deeding Holland's original homestead on Nowlin Creek in Jackson Hole to Campbell in 1896 for $500.[226]

Settler and hunting guide John Holland horse packing a grizzly bear hide out of the forest.
(Courtesy Jackson Hole Historical Society and Museum 1958.2814.001)

In October 1898, only a few years after gaining title to and selling his Jackson Hole property, Holland proved up on a 160-acre homestead under Desert Land Act on Horseshoe Creek in Teton Basin. In October 1900, he also obtained patent on a contiguous parcel by cash entry under the Homestead Act.[227] His address at the time was given as Haden, Fremont County, Idaho.[228] There was no Tom Foolery in Holland's processing his homestead claims in Teton Basin, it was accomplished in an efficient business-like manner.

Holland's homesteading and ranching in Teton Basin is further documented in a family history for Victor, Idaho, pioneer James Berger. When nineteen-year old Berger first came into Teton Basin in the spring of 1897, he was employed by Holland to cut logs and haul them by horse team from Twin Creek. The logs were used for the construction of buildings on John and Maud's 320-acre ranch, located at the mouth of Horseshoe Canyon. Holland paid Berger $20 a month for working from dawn-to-dusk, six days a week for two summers. Berger was given Sundays off to work on his own homestead cabin, and may have used Holland's horses for skidding his logs, too.[229] No one back then could have ever imagined a forty-hour work week.

Holland was raising horses and Carrington worked for him as a bronc buster. Holland was a witness on Carrington's Teton Basin Desert Entry Affidavit on June 5, 1901, giving his occupation as "rancher" and his residence as "Fremont County, Idaho."[230]

When Carrington first went to Jackson in 1898, he claimed he sometimes lived with Holland,[231] suggesting Holland was simultaneously maintaining residences in both Jackson Hole and Teton Basin. Carrington likely boarded at Holland's Horseshoe Creek Ranch at times, too.

Around this time, besides ranching, Holland was also guiding and
outfitting sport hunters. His obituary states: "As a cowboy he became
expert as a hunter and guide." Carrington recalled, "Holland had
some big hunters... a Boston shoe man, Count de Turin from Italy in
1900, Lord Morton Governor of India."[232]

Holland went back and forth from Teton Basin to Jackson Hole
guiding hunters; later, John may have even traveled back to Jackson
Hole from Oregon to guide.[233] A railhead at Scio, Oregon, made this
readily possible. The Oregon Short-Line Railroad (a subsidiary of the
Union Pacific) brought passengers as close as Market Lake (Roberts)
or St. Anthony, Idaho.

Another railroad line went to Livingston and Gardiner, Montana.
Guides would meet their clients at one of those places, and then take
them by horseback, buckboard, or wagon across Teton Pass from
Idaho or south through Yellowstone into the Jackson Hole country.
Several weeks or more were invariably involved in such hunting trips.

In 1898, Holland guided the Edwin B. Holmes party on a hunting
trip in the Blackrock-Togwotee Pass area, part of today's Teton
Wilderness. On that trip, they discovered a cave, actually a "sink" –
a hole in the limestone rock into which a stream drained, creating
an underground waterfall and underground channels. They named
it "Holmes Cave." The stream later became known as Holmes Cave
Creek. Holmes was a prominent shoe manufacturer in the Boston,
Massachusetts' area (likely the client Carrington mentioned).

In 1905, Holmes returned to further explore and map the cave.[234]
He invited Holland to join him on his return trip, but whether
Holland accompanied him isn't known. Holmes did, however, map
and name a feature of the cave after Holland: "Holland's Chamber."[235]

In September 1900, Teddy Roosevelt came through Rexburg, Idaho, on his Vice Presidential campaign. Carrington recollected, "John Holland, the old timer from Jackson, was living in Teton Basin ... we rode down to Rexburg – that's 35 miles. I was going to ride a bronc for [Roosevelt]...crowd was so thick...horse was scared to death and wouldn't even switch its tail ... Teddy done more for our Western country than any President ever done." [236] Holland must have been in agreement with the latter statement, too, for them to have ridden seventy miles on horseback to witness Roosevelt's stump speech.

Around this time, the Hollands realized livestock were suddenly missing from their Horseshoe Creek Ranch pasture. Holland traced the lost cattle to none other than Ed Harrington, who, after getting out of the Idaho State Penitentiary, was back living in Teton Basin. It seems Harrington was butchering his neighbor's beef and trying to pass it off as elk meat.

There was no friendship lost between the two men. Their paths in life had diverged. Holland had moved on to become a legitimate and well-respected Teton Basin rancher. He was well aware of Harrington's reputation as a thief. Harrington, in later testimony, declared Holland to be his "enemy." Harrington's grandson, John Watson, wrote in *The Real Virginian*, that in a confrontation, Holland fired a shot at Harrington which "just missed." Considering his years on the frontier, and his hunting and guiding experience, there is no doubt Holland had to be a skilled marksman; the miss was intentional – a warning shot.

Holland followed up by swearing out both a search and arrest warrant, leading to Harrington's arrest and, in 1901, landing him back in the Idaho State Penitentiary, convicted of grand larceny.

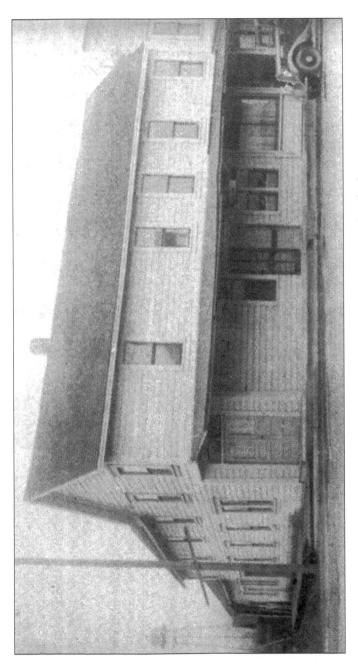

The Scio Hotel in the 1930s once owned by John and Maud Holland.
(Courtesy Carol Bates, Scio in the Forks of the Santiam, Albany Public Library, Oregon)

16
OREGON BECKONS –
JOHN AND MAUD MOVE ON ONCE MORE

After a few years, Maud's folks moved to Salem, Oregon…she wanted to be with her folks; then she and Holland moved there, too… I took down a [railroad] car load of horses and cattle for him.[237] – Enoch "Cal" Carrington

Not long after Harrington was convicted and sent to prison, Teton County, Idaho, land and deed records show John and Maud Holland sold their 320-acre Horseshoe Creek ranch property to Victor C. Hegsted of Salem, Oregon, for $8000 in 1902 – an enormous amount in those days. The value of their developed homestead ranch in Teton Basin had increased considerably over those of early-day Jackson Hole. A warranty deed was recorded by Hegsted on December 17 in Driggs, Idaho, that year.[238]

Before that sale, in 1901, the Hollands moved to Salem. Then, in 1903, they moved again, where they made homestead entry a short distance north of Scio in the Willamette Valley.[239] There is record of a John Holland homestead cash entry in Linn County, Oregon, on June 9, 1902, and another on December 1, 1904.[240] It appears to have been a period of growth and well being in the lives of the Hollands. Between the times of those homestead transactions, their second son, Glen, was born in 1903.

In 1905, John and Maud purchased and began operating the sixteen-room Scio Hotel.[241] On May 29, 1906, they suffered a tragic event. A fire raced out of control through an entire city block of the town.[242] While working to suppress the blaze, the hotel awning Holland was standing on collapsed and he fell into a window, badly cutting his foot. He continued fighting the fire despite his injury.

A few days later, a severe bacterial infection broke out in Holland's wound and swiftly spread up his leg. It was tetanus, generally known as lockjaw back then. Before the days of antibiotics little could be done. The gangrenous leg was amputated above the knee in an attempt to control the spread. Carrington recalled that Holland's leg was "amputated twice" in trying to stay ahead of the infection. Regardless, three doctors working in concert could not stop the incredibly rapid advance of inflammation. John Holland died at sunset on June 2, 1906. He was 51 years old.[243]

According to the obituary in the *Santiam News*, "Probably no one man exerted himself so energetically and persistently during the time of the fire, or had so much to do in preventing its spread, as did he. Suffice to say, he did his duty nobly, regardless of fatigue."

The *News* went on to say: "As a citizen, Mr. Holland enjoyed the fullest confidence of the townsmen and neighbors. As a husband and father he was most affectionate and kind… Seeing his duty he did it bravely and unflinchingly. Like a soldier going into battle, he did his duty to the utmost and in so doing laid down his life without a murmur."

Looking back on Holland's less civilized and lawless years in early-day Jackson Hole, some may find a certain redemptive irony in his membership with the Knights of Pythias, a brotherhood promoting "strict morality, absolute truthfulness, honor and integrity."
John Holland was buried one mile south of Scio in the Franklin

Butte Masonic Cemetery under the auspices of the Knights of Pythias, of which he was a member. "The grave," it was reported, "was literally covered from head to foot with the large number of floral offerings."[244]

Holland had traveled life's road a long way from his early years of trapping and living on the edge of the law in frontier Jackson Hole. His funeral service was one given for a well-liked and highly respected member of the community.

Holland's obituary briefly noted that he had been "in Wyoming for 20 years, where he worked in the stock business."[245] This statement would have no doubt been cause for a knowing wink and an ironic grin among the crusty frontier inhabitants of Jackson Hole who he had known and once lived among.

John Holland's life story indicates he was a respected, likeable, and highly capable individual. He displayed exceptional resourcefulness and drive, and had an apparent ability to charm all kinds of people – from frontier ruffians to dignitaries – in a diverse and challenging range of situations. Holland may have lived on the edge of the law out of necessity in his earliest Jackson Hole years, but in the end, he had grown into a model of respectability.

Maud Holland was left with two sons to raise, Edwin and Glen.[246] Two years later she leased the hotel to Will and Iva Abbott.[247] Maud died in 1937, at the age of 64, and was buried next to John. [248]

Downtown modern-day Jackson, Wyoming. (Courtesy of circumerostock.com)

EPILOGUE

Mavericks, homesteaders, trappers, big game guides, merchants, cowboys mixed with remittance men, wealthy hunters, dudes, and Easterners who came for unspoiled scenery – it was a blend that created a vigorous exciting community. A community unlike any other. – Fern K. Nelson, *This was Jackson's Hole.*

In 1922, during the Hollywood era of Western films, one of the early-day denizens of Jackson Hole hoped to cash in on his notoriety and perhaps become respectable. After a lifetime of being in and out of jail, desperado and thief Ed Harrington (Trafton) journeyed to Hollywood to sell his life story to the movie industry. However, in Los Angeles he died suddenly, not in a western saloon or a shootout, but from natural causes in an ice cream parlor. After someone found the embellished tale folded in his pocket, the *Los Angeles Times* ran the headline:

"The Virginian Dies Suddenly
– Owen Wister Novel Hero Was Real Pioneer –
Blazed First Trails Into Jackson Hole Country."

The fictional tale was Harrington's concluding epithet, a final irony in the roll call of Jackson Hole's first settlers.

Considering the choices Carnes and Holland faced in the early 1880s, traditional recognition of them as Jackson Hole's first settlers is a tribute to their mettle. Given that they are lauded as the "first white settlers" or "first permanent settlers" by historians, it is an enigma that as of this date, with the exception of Holland's Chamber in Holmes' Cave, there are no natural features or landmarks named after either one of them in Jackson Hole. Nor are there currently any signs, monuments, or historic interpretation on the National Elk

Refuge that tells their story or identifies the place of their original homesteads. Only an expanse of wind-worried grass marks the ground where they once pioneered.

The lives of Jackson Hole's early settlers were the prologue to the valley's rapid settlement and development. Once Euro-American settlement got a toe-hold, population surged. It grew from twenty frontiersmen in the 1880s to fifteen-hundred citizens in only twenty years. While Native American populations living off the land remained sustainably low for thousands of years, Euro-American settlers poured in at a whopping 740% increase in two decades, increasingly bringing civilization with them. Mormon settlers hoping to take up homesteads and prosper by farming and ranching made up a large percentage of the incoming settlers for a period of time after 1900.

Some early settlers came to this isolated high-mountain valley because they were escaping from a shady past and looking for a place to hide or to begin a new start; others came seeking the American dream of a land of milk and honey. Most discovered the valley to be a tough and challenging life. That there is a place in the valley known as "Poverty Flats" says it all.

Early residents of Jackson Hole took pride in their rough and rowdy reputations. Self-sufficiency, self-proclaimed toughness, and colorful characters were cherished. Their frontier lifestyle depended on year-round exploitation of the valley's abundant wildlife for subsistence and livelihood. To the European settlers, an abundance of wild ungulates indicated a potential for domestic stock grazing.

In 1916, Congress and President Woodrow Wilson authorized the Stock-Raising Homestead Act, allowing individuals to claim up to 640-acres, as compared to the earlier 160-acres through the

Homestead or Desert Entry Acts. This new law greatly assisted those settlers who sought to ranch.

A few homestead entries were filed to establish dude ranches, such as author and dude rancher Struthers Burt's renowned Bar-BC. The restored historic White Grass Ranch in Grand Teton National Park is representative of those early dude ranches. The course of Jackson Hole's future became set when it was recognized dude ranching generally paid better than farming and running cattle. With that realization undertakings to attract more people to the valley for outdoor recreation and the Old West ambiance followed. The valley's appeal for tourism and sport hunting obviously remains hugely successful today.

In the first-part of the twentieth century, some people who had no serious intention of farming or ranching made land entries simply to enjoy a lifestyle and to reside along the scenic mountain front within the shadow of the Teton Mountain ramparts. The homestead cabins existing at Cottonwood Creek, Taggart Lake, Lupine Meadows and Jenny Lake, which today comprise a designated Historic District in Grand Teton National Park, represent relic structures from that era. People today continue to be attracted to the valley for similar aesthetic reasons.

Wildlife's importance, particularly Jackson Hole's elk, was nationally recognized in 1912, when the National Elk Refuge was established through the government purchase of early settlers Robert and Grace Miller's ranchlands, which by then, through their industrious business dealings had grown to 1,760 acres.

Over decades, the approximately sixty-five original homesteads located immediately north of the town of Jackson, which today comprises the 25,000 acre National Elk Refuge, were acquired by the federal government.[249] Locals back then referred to the Elk Refuge as: "the government's ranch." The concern for conservation of Jackson Hole's wildlife continued to grow. Elk, along with the Tetons, became iconic symbols of Jackson Hole.

A large area immediately south of Yellowstone National Park, along with portions of the Teton Mountain Range received government protection from development in 1897 with the establishment of the Teton Forest Reserve. Those lands later became a part of the National Forest system. But Congress's subsequent attempts for a southern extension of Yellowstone National Park to include the Teton Range and northern parts of Jackson Hole were vigorously fought and defeated by the valley's citizens, particularly the ranchers, and state and local politicians.

In 1929, conservation proponents were successful in establishing a National Monument that included the central peaks of the Teton Range and some of the lakes along the foothills, an area encompassing one-third of Grand Teton National Park's present-day size. Later, homesteads that existed along the foot of the mountains, on the adjacent sagebrush flats, and around the lakeshores, were acquired by philanthropist John D. Rockefeller's Snake River Land Company. Robert Miller served as the procurement agent. After years of resistance by those opposed to the Park, the lands were finally donated to the federal government to expand Grand Teton National Park.

Some Wyoming and Jackson Hole residents felt betrayed by this maneuver. The fight in which Western Congressmen, the State of Wyoming, and some local residents and ranchers myopically, but determinedly, resisted the expansion of Grand Teton National Park went on for more than twenty years. Because of this stubborn political resistance, Grand Teton National Park as we know it today was only finally established in 1950.[250]

In recent decades, Teton County has been the fastest growing county in the State of Wyoming. The 2010 census of Jackson Hole showed a population growth of 17-percent over the previous decade, swelling the valley's population to 21,294 permanent residents.

No longer just an isolated farming and ranching community, today's inhabitants include, among others, world class athletes, outdoor enthusiasts, artists, writers, and entrepreneurs and wealthy individuals who find it prestigious to frequent Jackson Hole. As in the past, transients, opportunists, eccentrics, and shady and colorful characters are still attracted to the valley, too. Thanks to modern homes,technology, and transportation, over-wintering in the Hole has become much easier.

However, the resident population is only a part of today's story. Jackson Hole has become a year-round vacation destination. At last count, the valley boasted eleven bars, thirty art galleries, seventy-seven restaurants, more than eighty lodging properties (most of the restaurants and hotels have bars and serve liquor, too), twenty-nine real estate offices, and fifteen churches. Resort hotels, restaurants, and bars out number churches about ten to one. On any one day, seasonal encampment in the valley can exceed tens of thousands of visitors. Annually, millions of people from all over the world tour the valley to experience and view Jackson Hole's and Grand Teton National Park's scenery, wildlife, and pristine environs – a chance for them to feel awe for things represented by the natural world that are larger than themselves.

If the bachelor settlers of the 1880-1890s could see the Hole now, their jaws would hang agape in absolute astonishment at the sheer numbers of people and motor vehicles crowded into downtown Jackson at the peak of tourist season. And "Old Man Atherton" would no doubt have an apoplectic fit at the sight of the number of people at Jenny Lake on the Fourth of July nowadays, compared to the relatively few, which severely distressed him in the 1890s.

The Old West may be no more, but observing the landscape immediately north of the town of Jackson – across the open expanse of the National Elk Refuge and beyond into Grand Teton National Park and the Teton Mountain Range – the view today fills one with reflective nostalgia. Surely that vista of grand and open country appears much like it must have looked back when John Holland and Johnny Carnes first saw it more than a hundred years ago.

HOMESTEADING TERMINOLOGY

Claim jumper–Someone who knowingly and illegally occupies or uses land or property (mining claim, homestead) on which another person has already established a legal claim; more simply, a trespasser that intends adverse possession.

Cash homestead entry – An amendment to the Homestead Act that allowed for cash purchase of the land at $1.25 per acre after living on it for six months.

Desert Lands Act of 1877 – An act by Congress to promote development of arid to semi-arid lands public land in the western United States allowing entry and application for up to 320-acres if the necessary requirements were met and improvements were made. The improvements necessarily involved developing irrigation and producing agricultural crops. A Desert Entry could be made in addition to a homestead claim.

Free land – A misconception was/is that the Homestead Act provided "free land." Homesteading involved investment of time, labor, money, and negotiating the bureaucratic process in order to gain title. The land was not free. One advantage, however, was that taxes did not have to be paid on the property until title was obtained.

Homestead Act of 1862–It made public domain lands in the West available to be acquired by settlers for use as farms through a process of established requirements: build a house on it, reside on it continuously for five years, and cultivate a portion of it. "Those who had borne arms against the United States government" were disqualified, which eliminated everyone who served in the Confederate Army. The act was later amended to also allow purchase of the land for $1.25 per acre after staying for at least six months. Originally the Homestead Act applied to surveyed lands, but in 1880 it was modified to include unsurveyed land.

Homestead tract–Generally, 160-acres.

Final proof or proving up – Proving up required filing a notice of intent, paying fees, meeting all requirements, and filing final papers with the Land Office, wherein the claimant provided sworn testimony that he/she met all the requirements, and then having those statements collaborated by two or more witnesses. Witnesses were generally neighbors on adjoining tracts. The final paperwork or "proof" was sent to Washington, D.C.; then, if approved, a patent or title to the tract was issued.

Improvements – A livable dwelling was required. A barn, sheds, fencing, corrals, irrigation, clearing sagebrush and timber, and a percentage of the ground being brought under cultivation also qualified as improvements.

Manifest Destiny – The nineteenth century doctrine that Euro-American expansion and settlement of the West was predestined to be dominated by the United States. Congress viewed laws such as the Homestead Act as a part of that vision. The Homestead Act became an integral part of the westward movement and encouraged settlement.

Patent or title – A certificate of ownership. For Homestead and Desert Entries it was signed and approved by the President of the United States.

Pre-emption – A process enacted to accommodate settlers who had established themselves ahead of government surveyors. When the surrounding land was surveyed the squatter had the right to appear at the local land office and purchase up to 160-acres of their holdings for $1.25 per acre to pre-empt any other or subsequent claims, provided the settler could show proof of a dwelling and the required improvements to the land. The squatter's assumption was that their "legal right" to the land would eventually follow and be recognized.

Public domain– Land which is owned by the federal government. In the later part of the ninetieth and early twentieth centuries, such lands were generally open to private entry through an assortment of laws, such as the Homestead Act, Desert Lands Act, and Mining Act, all of which congress passed to encourage expansion of settlement and private economic development in the western states.

Relinquishment right – When a person has not yet acquired a title to the property, but sells their improvements along with their established right to a claim on a particular homestead property.

Squatter –A person who takes up residence on a property or on public domain lands without having ownership title, the assumption being that eventually their legal right or claim to the property will follow and be recognized.

Squatter's rights – A legal claim to property, in this case on federal public domain lands, based on a person living on it and making at least the minimum improvements necessary in accordance with requirements of the law.

Survey – A legally accepted and consistent method for describing land locations and boundaries.

Witnesses –A person who swears to the accuracy of the proof statements submitted to the local Land Office. Neighbors often witnessed each others' submissions.

NOTES

Preface Notes

1   Technically, the source of the Snake River begins as three small streams on the Two Ocean Plateau in the Teton Wilderness. These tributaries join in Yellowstone National Park. The headwaters includes all the streams and rivers that come together in the region to form the Snake River, such as the Buffalo Fork, Lewis River, Soda Fork, Gros Ventre River, Greys River, Salt River, Teton River, Henry's Fork, and others.

2   Dyke, J.C. *The West of the Texas Kid, 1881-1910: Recollections of Thomas E. Crawford.* Univ. of Oklahoma Press, Norman, 1962.

3   Diem K. and L. Diem. *A Community of Scalawgs, Renegades, Discharged Soldiers and Predestined Stinkers?.* Grand Teton Natural History Association, Moose, Wyoming, 1998. 198 p.

4   Wight, J.B. *The Jackson Hole Conspiracy.* Timbermill Press, Auburn, Wyoming, 2007. 251 p.

Chapter 1

1   Wright, G.A. *People of the High Country: Jackson Hole before Settlers.* Amer. Univ. Studies, Vol. 7, New York. 1984. 181p.

2   Wilson, C.A. *The Return of the White Indian Boy.* Univ. of Utah Press, Salt Lake City, Utah (bound with *The White Indian Boy* by Elijah N. Wilson), 1985.

3   Hardee, J. *Pierre's Hole! The Fur Trade History of Teton Valley, Idaho.* Sublette County Historical Society. Pinedale, Wyoming. 2010. 389 p.

4   An artist's rendition of a Native American encampment at Jackson Lake entitled *Indian Camp on Jackson Lake* by Hubert Collins may be viewed at the Grand Teton National Park's Colter Bay Museum. At one time, before Jackson Lake Dam, meadows existed at the north-end of Jackson Lake. It was a favorite place for encampment.

5   Cannon, K.P. and M.B. Cannon, "Jackson Hole Bison Dig: Results of 2004 Field Investigations." NPS Midwest Archaeological Center, Lincoln, Nebraska. 16p.

6   Frank Petersen wrote a brief commentary in *Recreation Magazine* saying he could snowshoe from his cabin and see bighorn sheep and elk. Rena Croft family papers, Lovell, Wyoming (pers. comm. 2012).
     '

7   Russell, Osborne, *Journal of a Trapper,* Aubrey L. Haines Ed., University of Nebraska Press, 1955. An excellent overview of Native Americans in the Greater Yellowstone is found in Thomas Turiano's *Select Peaks of Greater Yellowstone,* 2003.

Chapter 2
8   Mattes, M. J. *Colter's Hell and Jackson's Hole.* Chapter V. "Les Trois Tetons: The Golden Age of Discovery" National Park Service, et al., 1962.

9   Harris, B.1993. *John Colter, His Years in the Rockies.* Harris's map of Colter's alleged route south of Yellowstone shows him traveling through Jackson Hole and Pierre's Hole via Teton Pass. Other historians do not agree that Colter's route brought him that far south. See Hardee, op. cit. 2010.

10 Hardee, J. op.cit. 2010.

11 Ibid.

12 Ibid.

13 Ibid.

14 Mattes, M.J. VI. " Jackson's Hole: Era of the Rocky Mountain Fur Company." In *Colter's Hell & Jackson's Hole*. Natl. Park Service, et al. 1962.

15 Talbot, V.L. 1996. *David E. Jackson: Field Captain of the Rocky Mountain Fur Trade*. Jackson Hole Historical Society and Museum, Jackson, WY.

16 *History of Yellowstone Place Names,* edited by James S. Macdonald (2006) from Chittenden's book, *The Yellowstone National Park*.

17 Daugherty, J. op. cit. pp 36-38. National Park archaeologist Stephanie Crockett provides a map and discussion of prehistoric access routes into and out of Jackson Hole.

18 Talbot, op. cit. 1996.

Chapter 3
19 DeLacy, W. W. "A trip up the South Snake River in 1863," in: Daugherty, J. et al. Chapter 5, *A Place Called Jackson Hole*. Natl. Park Service, GTNP, Moose, Wyoming, 1999.

20 DeLacy, W.W. *Contributions to the Historical Society of Montana* 2, 1896. pp241-251.

21   Wight, J.B. op. cit. 2007, p154.

22   Daugherty, J. op. cit., pp 83-87.

23   Ibid, pp 86-87.

Chapter 4
24   Union Pass Interpretive Display @ www.*Ultimate Wyoming.com*.

25   Daugherty, op.cit. pp 68-70.

26   Hoyle, R.C. 1999. "To the Tetons by Train." CRM no.10, pp
     24-25.

27   According to J. Hardee (2010), the old Indian trail actually had
     several route variations involving Moose Creek, Mosquito Creek,
     and Mail Cabin Creek. It did not necessarily follow the location
     of today's highway over Teton Pass.
28   Daugherty, op. cit. p70.

29   Baillie-Grohman, W.A. *Camps in the Rockies,* Charles Scribner
     and Sons, New York (1882).

30   A good source document for the Doane Expepedition is: Orin
     H. and Lorraine J. Bonney. 1970. *Battledrums and Geysers: the
     Life and Journals of Lt. Gustaveous Cheney Doane.* Sage Books,
     Chicago.

31   Sanborn, M. *The Grand Tetons: The Story of the Men Who Tamed
     the Western Wilderness.* G.P. Putnam's Sons, NY (1978).

32   Known as the "Grand Controversy," it is still debated yet today
     whether or not Langford and Stevensonactually reached the

summit of the Grand; their claim was publicly challenged by William Owen in 1898.

33   Today local Teton Valley residents prefer to call the peak "Table Rock," but topographers and maps identify it as Table Mountain.

34   Hayden had many landscape features and places named after him over the course of his career besides that in Yellowstone, for example: six states have mountain peaks that were named after him and also the town of Hayden, Colorado. .

35   Daugherty, J. op.cit. p79.

Chapter 5
36   Bradford, F.. *Teton Jackson; The Life and Times of Jackson Hole's Famous Outlaw*. Mortimore Publishing, Lander, Wyoming, 2003. 102p.

37   Undated letter in the Edith Thompson Papers, Acc. No. 346. American Heritage Center, Laramie, WY. See also: Ken and Lenore Diem (1998), p32.

38   "Beaver Dick – The Mountain Man" (2007) and "A History about Beaver Dick," an interview conducted by Harold Forbush compliled by Vera Baldwin (1970) both posted on the World Wide Web.

39   Diem, K. and Lenore Diem, 1998, op.cit., pp32-33.

40   Thompson, E.N.S. *Beaver Dick, the Honor and the Heartbreak: A Historical Biography of Richard "Beaver Dick" Leigh*. Jelm Mountain Press, Laramie, Wyoming. 1982. 162p.

41   "An Elk Hunt at Two Ocean Pass in September 1892" by
      Theodore Roosevelt in *Century Illustrated Magazine*, Vol. XLIV,
      No. 6. Jackson Hole outfitter and guide, Harold Turner, believes
      Roosevelt actually met up with Dick Leigh and his family at the
      Snake River Meadows near, but not actually at, Two Ocean Pass
      (pers. comm.. w/author, 2012).

42   Anderson, J. "Proving Up," in: *Spindrift: Stories of Teton Basin*,
      pp 45-54. On p 50, Dale Breckenridge describes Tim Hibbert
      as "infamous," reportedly having escaped from jail in Kansas.
      Cal Carrington mentions a Hibbert in one of his interviews,
      too, saying Hibbert was involved in rustling stock at the head of
      the Green River and "pushing them into Jackson Hole;" if true,
      perhaps into Teton Basin, too. Also, Stone, E.A. *Uinta County:
      Its Place in History* (1924) mentions a trapper by the name of
      Tim Hibbard, who supposedly over-wintered in Jackson Hole in
      1865. It's not known if they are all the same person.

43   Wight, J.B. op.cit, p25. Also Lt. Gustavus Doane in his 1876
      winter expedition recorded that trapper John Pierce was living
      at the south-end of Jackson Hole in a crude cabin. Pierce gave
      the Doane party a quarter of an elk. Dick Leigh also mentions
      trapper John Pierce being in Teton Basin in September 1876, in
      Beaver Dick: The Honor and the Heartbreak, pp68-70.

44   Daugherty, op.cit. p90.

45   Ibid.

46   Pers. Comm. with Dale Breckenridge (David's grandson),
      Tetonia, Idaho, 2012.

47 Anderson, J. 2000. "Proving Up," *Spindrift: Stories of Teton Basin*, Teton Arts Council Anthology, pp 45-54.

48 Pers. Comm. Dale Breckenridge, Tetonia, Idaho, 2012.

49 Sanborn, op.cit.

Chapter 6
50 Anderson, op.cit.

51 Wight, J. B, op.cit.

52 Righter,R.W. *A Teton Country Anthology.* Roberts Reinhart, Inc. 1990. pp45-56.

53 Calkins, F. *Jackson Hole*, Alfred A. Knopf, New York. 1973.

Chapter 7
54 Daugherty, op.cit. p90. Some sources give the date as 1883, such as in Fern Nelson's *This Was Jackson's Hole* (p13), but generally 1884 appears more commonly. Daugherty comments that there are discrepancies with the 1884 date, but nevertheless uses it for when "permanent settlement" began. The 1884 date is contradicted by a number of incidents and records. The romanticized histories of Jackson Hole's settlement are more myth than fact, e.g. see: Betts, R.B. 1978. *Along The Ramparts of the Tetons.* Bachelor settler Mike Detweiler(or Detwiler), for example, also took up a homestead along Flat Creek in 1883, too, just north of Carnes, but is generally not credited as being among the "founding fathers." While no BLM GLO records were found for Detweiler obtaining a patent, one source does say he received a patent in 1900. USF&WS National Elk Refuge files, cited in Smith, et.al. *Imperfect Pasture*, shows he sold or

relinquished his homestead to Robert Miller.

55   Daugherty, p90.

56   Ibid. p80.

57   Nelson, F. *This was Jackson's Hole.* High Plains Press, Glendo, Wyoming, 1994, p14.

58   Ibid.

59   Smith, B., E. Cole, and D. Dobkin. *Imperfect Pasture.* U.S. Fish and Wildlife Service National Elk Refuge and Grand Teton Natural History.Association, Jackson, Wyoming, 2004. p7.

60   Nelson, F. op. cit. p19.

61   Ibid, p14. Also see: *Jackson Hole Courier* 5/20/1954, "It Happened Long Ago."(in Jackson hole historical Society and Museum "Settler's file," Jackson, Wyoming.

62   Daugherty, op.cit. pp 91 & 147.

63   Will Simpson, wrangler for Pap Conant's posse in 1885, noted that two cabins existed which belonged to Holland and Carnes.

64   Diem, K. and L. Diem, op. cit., 1998, provides well-researched descriptions of some of the rough characters who inhabited the Jackson's Hole-Teton Basin area in the early years.

65   Lt. Doane's journal describing his 1876 winter expedition through Jackson Hole. (He reconstructed his journal after losing the original when his boat capsized in the Snake River Canyon.)

66 July 16, 1931 obituary: "Pioneer Civil War Vet Passes…"
    Box 2, Owen Collection (from the personal files of Loraine
    Bonney, Kelly, Wyoming). Also: Official Roster of the Soldiers
    of the State of Ohio in the War of the Rebellion, 1861-1866,
    Vol. XI, Akron, OH, 1891 (on file at the JHHS&M, Jackson,
    Wyoming).

67 Nelson, F. op. cit. p13.

68 Sommers, J. *Green River Drift: A History of the Upper Green River
    Cattle Association.* Sky House Publishing, Helena, Montana,
    1994. p2.

69 Ibid, p13. Also: Calkins, F. 1973. *Jackson Hole.* Alfred A. Knopf,
    New York. p129. The author also searched Wyoming GLO
    records and found no record of a filing or patent, which supports
    the belief Carnes relinquished his Fontenelle claim.

70 On a June 1901 Affidavit of Witness for Enoch Carrington's
    Desert Entry in Teton Basin, No. 3116,Holland gives his age
    as 46 years, National Archives case file; also, *Santiam News*
    June 1906 obituary. In Carol Bates, c1989, *Scio in the Forks of
    the Santiam*, Gates Graphics, Scio, OR. p275, where his death
    certificate shows his birth date as December 14, 1854; and, Pre-
    Emption Proof – Testimony of Claimant filed in Lander GLO
    April 16, 1894. Holland testified he was native born in Missouri
    (National Archives case file). Also see Bates, op.cit. p275.

71 John H. Holland certificate of death, June 3. 1906. Scio,
    Oregon, in Bates (op.cit.) and U.S. 1900 Federal Census
    (Ancestry.com)

72 *Santiam News* June 1906 obituary, op.cit., p275.

73 A bullwhacker for the Union Pacific railroad construction is
    not as innocuous as it may appear. Bullwhackers involved in
    the construction of the Union Pacific railroad were a rough lot.
    The construction camps they worked out of were notoriously
    known as "Hell on Wheels," consisting of crude shacks, tents,
    and bars frequented by gamblers, prostitutes, and other camp
    followers. See: Dary, D. *The Oregon Trail* (2004), pp304-306.
    Nelson, F. op.cit. provides considerable information on Holland
    and Carnes, however, the Jackson Hole Historical Society and
    Museum sources she cites ("Betty Hayden Interviews") could
    not be verified or located. Robertson, M.E.W. *The First Families
    Into Jackson Hole* (gathered from Wilson family and compiled by
    Judith Anderson). Jackson Library Special Collection, Jackson,
    Wyoming.

74 It was not confirmed that this was our John H. Holland, but
    appears highly probable. The case file for the entry was not
    reviewed, only the GLO IDIDAA013924 record. Cash sale entry
    sometimes may not have any personal identifiers in the record.
    The legal location of the homestead was: NE Sec. 16, T16S,
    R40E, Boise Meridian.

75 Nelson, F. p19: Albert Richards chanced to become acquainted
    with trapper John Holland in the early 1880s in southwestern
    Wyoming, who told Albert about Jackson Hole;" also p14,
    stating that Holland was present and active in the La Barge
    Creek area of Wyoming.

Chapter 8
76 Daugherty, op. cit. p147.

77 Sommers, J. op.cit. pp3-5.

78 Carrington filed an April 1897 water right claim for "surplus
    waters from John Holland's spring." Teton County, Idaho,
    courthouse land and water records. Teton Valley was called Teton
    Basin back then. It includes parts of Wyoming and Idaho.
    Layser, E. F. *I Always Did Like Horses and Women: Enoch Cal
    Carrington's Life Story* (2008), p67. See also: Gillette, W. 1979.
    "The Memorable Character – Cal Carrington." A Quarterly of
    Idaho History, Snake River Echoes, Vol. 8:3.

79 Bonney, O.H. and L.G. Bonney. 1972. *Bonney's Guide: Grand
    Teton National Park and Jackson's Hole.* Trip 12. Houston, Texas.
    pp 122-123.

80 Carrington's 1957 interview was conducted at the University of
    Wyoming by Clifford Hansen (American Heritage Center tape
    transcribed by Bonney and Bonney). Tim Hibbert is described
    in *Spindrift: Stories of Teton Basin*, p50, as "infamous." He was
    known locally for having escaped from a Kansas jail, for having
    rustled horses, and for long-distance horseback riding. He
    resided in Teton Basin before the 20th century began.

81 Ibid. Enoch Cal Carrington 1957 Interview.

82 Calkins, F. op.cit., p129. The primary source Calkins refers to
    is the William L. Simpson Collection at the Western History
    Research Center at the University of Wyoming, Laramie. Some
    sources state the cattle were owned by both Holland and Carnes,
    others include Mike Detweiler. Kenneth and Lenore Diem in
    *A Community of Scalawags, Renegades, Discharged Soldiers and
    Predestined Stinkers*(1998) cite Van Derveer, N. c1939 "Early
    Settlement" (American Heritage Center, Laramie), who state,
    "…100 head of cattle were driven over Teton Pass by Holland in
    1883." It's unlikely, however, that Holland would have obtained

100 head of cattle from anywhere on the Idaho side of the Pass in 1883. The first Mormon pioneers only arrived there around that time. Given the large number of cattle on the Green River, and Holland and Carnes familiarity with that area, it seems more likely the cattle were brought in from there. Daugherty (1999) states that Carnes, Holland and Detweiler owned the 100 head of cattle.

83   Pap Conant was a frontiersman from Lander, Wyoming, who survived an Indian fight where he was shot through the body. The Conant trail from Teton Basin into Jackson Hole is not named after him, however; rather Dick Leigh named the trail after Al Conant who came to the Tetons in 1865 (see Diem, op. cit., p32).

84   Calkins, op. cit. p115.

85   Simpson implies that the posse questioned Carnes and Holland about their business in the Hole and received the reply: "trapping." Trapping appeared to have been a euphemism encompassing a wide-range of frontier activities.

86   Calkins, op. cit. p115.

87   Ibid, (from the William Simpson collection).

88   Driggs, B.W. 1970 ed. *History of Teton Valley, Idaho.* Arnold Agency, Rexburg. Idaho.

89   Driggs, Ibid and The Idaho State Historical Society Reference Series, "Teton" Jackson, #451.

90   The reports of Teton Jackson's whereabouts are sketchy. The

Cooper killing in Teton Basin allegedly took place in February 1884. Jackson and Thompson were acquitted of the murder. Subsequently, Teton Jackson was arrested in Montana and returned to Idaho where he was found guilty of horse rustling. He supposedly escaped from the Boise Penitentiary after a few months (in 1885). Newspaper reports of his escape, however, are from 1888. Rumor says he passed through Jackson Hole after his escape, then moved to Lander and became respectable.

91   Bradford, E. 2003. *Teton Jackson: The Life and Times of Jackson Hole's Famous Outlaw.* Mortimore Publishing, Lander, Wyoming. 102p.

92   Idaho State Historical Society Reference Series, "Teton "Jackson, #451.

93   "History of Uinta County" (c1917) at www.wyominggeneology.com

94   Bradford, op.cit.

95   Ibid.

96   The *Cheyenne Daily Leader*, Oct. 12, 1866, in: Platts, D. 2004. *Robert Miller: An Enigma.* Wilson, Wyoming. p3.

97   Ibid. Also: Bradford, 2003, p 48.

98   Calkins, op. cit. p129.

99   Carrington 1957 interview, op. cit.

100   Bonney's Guide, op. cit. 1972.

101 Platts, D. 2004. *Robert Miller:An Enigma..* Self-Published, Wilson, Wyoming. 39p.

102 Mumey, N. *The Teton Mountains: Their History and Tradition.* Aircraft Press, Denver (1947).

103 Calkins, op. cit. p115.

104 Wister, O. 1902. *The Virginian.* Macmillan Co., NY. pp304-305.

Chapter 9
105 Owen, W. 1892. *Bill Barlow's Budget,* 9 June. Reprinted in Jackson Hole Historical Society and Museum Chronicle, Fall 2006.

106 Owen, W. op. cit. p147.

107 Nelson, F. op. cit. pp34-39.

108 Various published sources.

109 Pre-emption proof testimony in National Archives WYWYAA022417 case file.

110 Daugherty, op. cit. p168.

111 Nelson, F. op. cit. p109.

112 Memories of Charles W. Hedrick." Unpublished mimeo, November 1, 1948, 28 p.

113 Excerpted and paraphrased from: *The Ballad of Dick Turpin* by Alfred Noyes. www.allpoetry.com/poem.

114 Pers. Comm. w/Robert Rudd, 2012. Rudd personally knew "Stippy" Wolff (Emil's son) and his family.

115 Daugherty, op.cit. pp 90-91.

116 Ibid, p96.

117 Rudd, op.cit. Rudd was personally told this by Emil's son, Stippy.

118 Daugherty, p96.

119 Platt, D. *John Cherry (1853-1931): One of Jackson Hole's Earliest Settlers.* Bearprint Press, Jackson (1991). 134 p. The number of cattle he owned in 1895 is found in Daugherty, p 49.

120 Kreps, B. *Windows to the Past: Early Settlers in Jackson Hole.* Jackson Hole Historical Society and Museum, 2006. pp 1-3.

121 It's unlikely this was a spur of the moment arrangement. It would seem more likely that the Wilson-Cheney party would not have risked arriving late in the season in Jackson Hole without some prior arrangements. Members of the Wilson-Cheney party may have ridden ahead earlier and set up the arrangements with Holland, Carnes, and Cherry in advance. Holland had a 17'x17' cabin and it is not likely that he and all the others would have spent the winter together in it. Holland must have used another nearby place for temporary residence or possibly Teton Basin.

122 Memoir of Mrs. Ervin Wilson (Mary Jane Lucas) in Platts, D. *John Cherry (1853-1931): One of Jackson's Earliest Settlers* (1991). Bearprint Press, Jackson. 134p.

123 Betts, R.B. *Along the Ramparts of the Tetons.* Colorado Associated University Press, Boulder,1978. pp148-149.

124 Ibid., p 149.

125 Robertson, op. cit. 1990, pp 2-5. See comment in note 108 above.

126 Nelson, F. p16. Whether Carnes and Holland moved out, moved over, or were temporarily out of the Valley isn't known. It seems likely for the 1896 date, at least, Holland would have moved over to his Teton Basin property. While Holland is given credit for use of the cabin and stable, Maud Carpenter, in fact, owned it at the time. It's likely Holland and Carnes rented or leased out their cabins. Historian Nelson also said Will Crawford moved out temporarily, giving up his property for two years. No doubt he leased it out, too. Other established settlers also helped the Mormon arrivals. John Cherry let them use his homestead; Miller sold them hay.

127 Daugherty, op.cit. p 140. 128

128 Pers. Comm. with former Jackson Hole Historical Society Director Robert Rudd, who heard it described by Slim Lawrence; and also as was also told in an interview by former Wyoming Senator Cliff Hansen with Pattie Layser published in *Teton Home Magazine* (2004).

Chapter 10
129 Sources for Moses Giltner's biographic material include: *Progressive Men of Wyoming* (1901), p 819; John Daugherty, *A Place Called Jackson Hole* (1999); and, Robert Betts, *Along the Ramparts of the Tetons* (1978). Jack Huyler's *And That's the*

Way it Was (2003), pp 140-151, contains contradictory, if not erroneous, information on Giltner. Huyler's stories about Giltner are entertaining, but seem to be based on town gossip.

130 William Manning's biographic history was obtained from a number of sources: *Progressive Men of Wyoming*; Brigham Madsen's *The Northern Shoshone* (2000) and *The Bannock War of 1895* (1955); John Daugherty's *A Place Called Jackson Hole* (1999); Jermy Wight, *The Jackson Hole Conspiracy, 1895* (2007); "Memories of Charles W. Hedrick," unpublished mimeo (1948); and on-line websites: www.wyomingtalesandtrails.com and www.rootsweb.ancestry.com/ – wytetotp/bios1.htm. His obituary may be found in the August 25,1932 Pinedale Roundup Newspaper, Pinedale, Wyoming, p1.

131 Robert Miller's biographic information was constructed primarily from: Doris B. Platts, *Robert E. Miller: An Enigma* (2003); John Daugherty, *A Place Called Jackson Hole* (1999), and Fern Nelson, *This Was Jackson's Hole* (1994).

132 Frank Petersen's biographic history was produced from an unpublished two-page biography constructed by his son Charlie Petersen, provided by his granddaughter Rena Croft; and personal communication with Rena. Other sources included: John Daugherty, *A Place Called Jackson Hole* (1999); Jermy Wight, *The Jackson Hole Conspiracy, 1895* (2007); Fern Nelson, *This Was Jackson's Hole*, 1994; and Doris Platts, *The Cunningham Ranch Incident* (1992).

Chapter 11
133 Platts, D.B. *The Cunningham Ranch Incident of 1892*. Wilson, Wyoming, 1992. 161p.

134 Driggs, B. *History of Teton Valley*. Caxton Printers, Ltd. Caldwell,
     Idaho, 1926. p129. Driggs says it was Carnes who led the
     men across the Pass on snowshoes, not Holland. Driggs also
     says Carnes was first sent to investigate the men with horses
     in Jackson Hole by Idaho Sheriff Swanner. However, Swanner
     is never mentioned in Jackson Hole accounts of the incident.
     Driggs's recording of the incident and persons involved differs
     substantially from Platts' detailed research.

135 Platts, op. cit. 1992, pp134-137. The participants appear to
     have later purposely confounded who all was involved through
     conflicting stories. John Carnes 1931 obituary (No. 94, Owen
     Collection) states: "At one time he was deputy sheriff ... sent to
     disperse a band of horse thieves that infested the region. As he
     always expressed it, 'We were sent in after them, and they are
     there yet.'"

136 Platts, p95, presents strong evidence for a connection between
     Butch Cassidy's capture in nearby Star Valley just eight days
     before the Cunningham Incident, stating: "Both events were
     part of a determined effort by Montana stockmen." The same
     regulators were involved and they recovered horses from both
     places belonging to the same Montana ranchers.

137 Platts provides a comprehensive and well-researched treatment of
     the incident.

138 Minutes of the April 26, 1892, Uinta County Commissioner's
     meeting, p540 (in: Platts, p116). Cal Carrington in his 1957
     interview claimed Holland was friends with a civic leader
     named Rathburn in Evanston possibly from when Holland had
     earlier lived in the Green River area, and that Rathburn was
     instrumental in getting Holland appointed Justice of the Peace.

139 Platts, p110.

140 Enoch Cal Carrington interview, op.cit.

141 Bonney, O.H and L.G. Bonney. *Bonney's Guide: Grand Teton National Park and Jackson's Hole*. Houston, TX (Trip 12), 1972. pp122-23. The plaintiff's first name appears to have been lost to time. Only the surname West is known from the Carrington interview.

142 Kenneth and Lenore Diem, op. cit. p95.

Chapter 12
143 Bradford, op.cit. Bradford wrote that Ed Harrington and Teton Jackson worked together commercial meat hunting at the southwest corner of Yellowstone Park, smoking game meat and then shipping it to Salt Lake City.

144 Layser, E.F. "The Original Natural Setting of Pierre's Hole – A Changed and Changing Landscape." In*: Spindrift:Stories of Teton Basin*. Teton Arts Council, Driggs, Idaho, 2000. pp18-23.

145 Daugherty, op. cit. p133.

146 Synder, G. *The Practice of the Wild*. Counterpoint, Berkley, California, 1900. pp 27-51. Also called "Tragedy of the Commons;" the idea is explained by Garret Hardin (1968).

147 The "commons" embraces all creations of Nature and society that we inherit jointly and freely, and hold in trust for future generations. In the example of the American bison, commercial hide and meat hunters, sport hunters, and government policies all converged, each intent on their own purposes, destroying

the vast herds, slaughtering hundreds of thousands of bison in a decade, and bringing about near the extinction of the animal.

148 Anderson, A.A. 1933. *Experiences and Impressions.* MacMillian Co, NY.

149 "Memories of Charles W. Hedrick, op.cit..

150 Daugherty, op. cit. p298. "There was much game wasted [by whites] in those days"… recalling anything but a conservation ethic… statement by Mary White.

151 "An Elk Hunt at Two Ocean Pass in September 1892' by Theodore Roosevelt, *Century Illustrated Magazine*, Vol. XLIV, No. 6. (Republished in many sources, the latest in: *The Wilderness Hunter* … Sterling Publishing, Barnes and Noble Edition (2012).

152 Illustrated by the State Auditor's letter to the Lander *Sun Leader* in Wight, J. (2007), pp 82-85; and Ida Simpson's letter on p87 stating she observed a band of Bannocks on Union Pass with "300 elk hides."

153 Wight, J. pp 28-29.

154 Ibid. Manning's testimony at federal hearings after the episode.

155 Ibid., p 30.

156 Stone, E. A. *Uinta County: Its Place in History*, (1924).

157 The men in the posse commanded by William Manning were: J.G.Fisk, Ham Wort, Steve Adams, Joe Calhoun, Willam

Crawford, Martin Nelson, Joe Enfinger, W. Munger, Ed Hunter, Frank Woods, Frank Petersen, Jack Shive, Georde Madison, Andrew Madison, Mose Giltner, Charles Estes, George Wilson, John Wilson, Irv Wilson, Victor Gustavese, Steve Leek, William Bellue and John Cherry (from Wight, *Jackson Hole Conspiracy*, p34).

158 Wight, p167. It's not clear if Miller's reference to "forted up at my place,"was in reference to Marysvale or a separate gathering at his ranch.

159 Ibid. Wight presents detailed documentation of the build up of events, correspondence, telegrams, and personalities involved throughout the episode.

160 Ibid. A copy of Robert Miller's letter is found on p 132.

161 After all the newspaper hype, it appears from other reports that the Lander posse which arrived in Jackson Hole with Sheriff Grimmett may have been comprised of only fourteen men, not a "well-mounted 100." Six members of the Lander posse pilfered homestead cabins in the valley. They were referred to as "tinhorns" in a Market Lake telegram and a *Sun Leader* piece, in which it appears William Arnn is incorrectly referred to as "Henry Carns" (Wight, p 185). Will Simpson's journal is cited by other historians identifying the person as Arnn.

162 Wight, Ibid.

163 Ibid.

164 Ibid. p 185. See above. The incident has been documented in several Jackson Hole histories, but not inthe context of the

Indian War or that it was Lander posse members who pilfered homestead cabins.

165 Betts, op. cit. p157.

166 Allen, M.V. *Early Jackson Hole*. Press Room Printing, Redding, California, 1981. pp 253-254.

167 A report by an investigating U.S. Deputy Marshal condemned the whole affair, saying he found no evidence of game slaughter by the Indians and that the killing of Indians was premeditated and prearranged, intended to stir up trouble and get federal troops sent into the area in order to shut the Indians out. He concluded that it was useless to attempt a hearing or trial because no local or state officials would hold Manning's posse responsible (see Wight, pp 202-204). For versions of the affair that are sympathetic to the white settler's position, see: F. Nelson, *This Was Jackson's Hole*, pp 137-140, and Marion Allen, *Early Jackson Hole*, pp243-254. Both authors of those accounts were long-time Jackson Hole residents.

168 Wight, pp 69-79.

169 Ibid., pp200-201.

170 Layser, E.F. *Green Fire: Stories from the Wild* (2010), pp 190-234. State geologist, David Love, claimed bison existed in the Red Desert up until the 1950s. The state did nothing to protect them. Bison were never given game animal status in Wyoming and therefore could be hunted anytime.

Chapter 13
171 Jacoby, K. *Crimes against Nature: Squatters, Poachers, Thieves*

and the Hidden History of America. Univ. of California Press, California, 2001.

172 Anderson, A.A. 1933. *Experiences and Impressions.* MacMillian Co., NY.

173 Wight, op. cit. p205.

174 Nelson, op.cit.p 140.

175 Daugherty, op. cit. pp 93-94.

176 Nelson, pp 141-144.

177 Allen, op. cit. p212

178 Bradford, op. cit.

179 Ibid., pp 298-300; also see Kreps' (2006) account of local game warden Si Ferrin, pp 53-54.

180 Daugherty, p299; also see Allen, pp5-12, where the Glidden letters criticizing game management in Jackson Hole that were published in *Outdoor Life* in 1902 are reproduced.

181 Irland, F. "The Wyoming Game Stronghold." *Scribner's Magazine,* Vol. 34: no. 3 (1903), pp258-276.

182 Kenneth and Lenore Diem, op. cit. pp 97-118.

183 Ibid., p 100.

184 Daughtery, op. cit. p300.

185 Nelson, p155.

186 Diem, pp97-118.

187 Ibid., p111.

188 Daughtery, p300. Daugherty identifies the three men who
     confronted Brinkley and Purdy as: Charles Harvey, Bill Menor
     and Charles Harvey. Allen, p212, says one of the men was Jim
     Budge. Like the Cunningham Cabin incident participants,
     the true identities of vigilante committees was probably never
     revealed. Kenneth and Lenore Diem, p104, state: "Many
     different men were reported as being part of the vigilantes group,
     so it is confusing as to who all went to Binkley's ranch that
     night."

189 Diem, p 104.

190 Ibid., p 105.

191 Ibid., p 109.

192 Ibid., pp 110-111.

193 Ibid., p 113.

194 Ibid., pp 111-118.

195 Layser, E.F. 2008, op.cit. p47.

196 Betts, op. cit. p176.

Chapter 14

197 The Hibbert family letters in J. Anderson's "Proving Up," *Spindrift*, 2000 (op. cit.), p46.

198 Dyke, J. *The West Texas Kid, 1881-1910: Recollections of Thomas E. Crawford*. Univ. of Oklahoma Press, 1962.

199 Daughtery, op. cit. p 204.

200 Smith, et al. *Imperfect Pasture* (op. cit.), Figure 1 and Appendix C (2004).

201 Daughtery, p205.

202 Diem, K., L.Diem, and W. Lawrence. *A Tale of Dough Gods, Bear Grease, Cantaloupe and Sucker Oil.* University of Wyoming-National Park Service Research Center, Moran, Wyoming, 1986. pp 24-25.

203 Smith, et al. *Imperfect Pasture*, op.cit., pp 7 & 147.

204 National Archives Case Files, BLM GLO Land Patent Details for John Carnes WYWYAA033418, Document 91 and John Holland WYWYAAO22417, Document 35.

205 Nelson, op. cit. p16.

206 Platts, D. *John Cherry: His lies, Life and Legend.* Bearpaw Press, Jackson, Wyoming, 1991.

Chapter 15

207 John Carnes' homestead patent is on display at the JHHS&M in Jackson, Wyoming. (See also page 160.)

208 From research of Teton County, Wyoming, courthouse land
    records conducted by U.S. Fish and Wildlife Service, National
    Elk Refuge, volunteer historian William Chaney. The National
    Archives case file for Carnes' homestead entry was not obtained,
    but it might shed additional light on dates, improvements and
    serve as an important comparison to Holland's preemption
    testimony.

209 Carrington, 1957 interview. Carrington was also interviewed
    in Teton Valley in 1958 by Dwight Stone, where he told this
    same story. The 1958 interview tape is on file at Teton Valley
    Museum, Driggs, Idaho.

210 Nelson, op.cit., p16.

211 John Carnes Obituary, July 16, 1931 (no. 94, Box 2, Owen
    Collection).

212 National Archives Case File, BLM-GLO WYWYAA022417.

213 This was about a month after the preemption filing and
    Holland could not have received title yet at that time even
    though he deeded the property to Maud. Some say he sold a
    relinquishment right.

    The property was transferred by deed #10805 drawn up and
    executed in Fremont County, Idaho, June 16, 1894. In *Imperfect
    Pasture* (Figure 1 and Appendix C) Maud and John are each
    shown to own separate but adjoining homesteads.

214 Ibid.

215 Don C. Driggs was an important citizen of early-day Teton

Valley. He owned and operated the first mercantile store in Driggs, Idaho, and the town was named after him.

216 Daugherty, p93.

217 William Crawford and John Hicks were both early-day homesteaders who located along Flat Creek just north of today's town of Jackson. Miller eventually bought Hick's homestead (op. cit. *Imperfect Pasture*).

218 Carnes' 1877 date is consistent with when they reportedly first met in the Green River area. Miller's date 1886 date conflicts with Arnn's testimony that both men over wintered in the Hole in 1885, as well as other histories.

219 National Archives Case File WYWYAA022417, Document 35, Testimony of Claimant and Witnesses.

220 Ibid.

221 Land and patent records, Teton County, Idaho, courthouse. Carrington uses Enoch or E.C. Carrington instead of Cal for a signature on early documents.

222 In the Teton County, Wyoming, land records, Maud uses her maiden name, Carpenter, in 1894 and 1896. But in the 1902 sale of their Teton Valley, Idaho, Horseshoe Creek Ranch, she uses her married name, Holland.

223 Ancestry.com. and 1900 U.S. Federal Census.

224 Franklin Butte Cemetery records and Linn County, Oregon June 1906 *Santiam News* obituary (cited in: Carol Bates, *Scio In The*

Forks of the Santiam, p275). The 1894 marriage date is given in
Holland's obituary and also in the 1900 U.S. Federal Census.
Previously, sources state they married in the "late 1890s." The
name usage on deeds raises the question if they were ever legally
married. Perhaps when they needed witnesses to the signing of
documents and deeds, she used the name most knew her by at
the time, Carpenter. By the 1900s, people in Teton Basin knew
them both under Holland's name. In any case, it was wise in
those times to claim to be married, forget anything as serious as
rustling or poaching, arrests were made for adultery (see p 93,
Kenneth and Lenore Diem, op.cit.).

225 Delayed birth certificate, case#12938/41963, Oregon State Archives.

226 Teton County, Wyoming, courthouse land records. According to
the records, John Holland transferred his Jackson Hole Nowlin
Creek homestead to Maud just before they were married. She
in turn, a few years later, in 1896, sold it to Campbell using her
maiden name. Perhaps it simplified the transaction, since she
owned it under her maiden name of Carpenter.

227 National Archives Case Files, BLM GLO records
IDIDAA048996, Document 819 and IDIDAA048997,
Document 3074. Homestead patent #3074.

228 U.S.1900 Federal Census.

229 History of James Henry Berger, 6p. Unpublished Berger family
history, Courtesy Ron Berger and family, Troy, ID. The 1900
U.S. Census shows an 18 year old Fred Watson living with the
Holland's, he was likely employed as a ranch hand.

230 National Archives Case File for Enoch C. Carrington's Desert

Entry No. 3116.

231 Ibid. This statement would seem to indicate Holland still had a place of residence in Jackson Hole after sale of his homestead to Maud and her transfer of it to George Campbell in 1896.

232 Carrington 1957 interview, op.cit.

233 Nelson, op. cit. p18. Also: Carrington in his 1957 interview mentioned he returned from his Forest Service work to guide hunters with John Holland in 1908.

234 Nelson, Ibid. In addition, USDA Forest Service Blackrock Ranger Station documents contain information regarding the cave and its discovery. Holmes was a charter member of the Brookline, Massachusetts, Norumbega Fraternity Lodge and was said to be "a man of prestigious ancestry." www. norumbegafraternity.org.

235 Ibid. Also: Chris Hill, etal. *Caves of Wyoming*. Geol. Survey of Wyoming, University of Wyoming, Laramie. Bull. 59 (1976), pp 347-351.

236 Carrington 1957 interview, op.cit.

Chapter 16
237 Carrington 1957 interview. Scio had its own railroad depot (in Bates, op.cit.).

238 Deed Book 3, p75&80, Driggs Courthouse, Teton County, Idaho. After taking up residence, Hegsted apparently performed marriages in Fremont County, Idaho. He married James Berger and Dessa Parsons in 1905 (History of James Berger, op.cit.).

239 Carrington, in his interview, said they moved to Salem . Nelson,
     F. op.cit., p17, said they moved to Socio, Linn County, Oregon.
     The Hollands moved first to Salem and then two years later, in
     1903, to a farm in Socio.

240 National Archives Case File, BLM GLO OROCAA043219,
     Document 7028 and OROCAA 047181, Document 7514,
     respectively. The case files were not obtained, but might be
     valuable in further contributing to the complete story of the
     Holland's life in Oregon.

241 Bates, C. *Scio in the Forks of the Santiam* (c1989), pp 273 &275

242 Details about the fire are found in the *Oregon Statesman*, May,
     1906; and. also the *Albany Democrat*, June 1906.

243 Bates, p275. Holland's *Santiam News* obituary is included,
     entitled: "Death of John Holland.". His son Glen said, it was
     "lockjaw." Carrington in his 1957 interview incorrectly stated
     Holland was "65 years old" at the time.

244 Ibid.

245 Bates, op.cit.One son was named Glen A. Holland (1903-
     1976). He served as the U.S. Navy in WWII and is also buried
     in Franklin Butte Cemetery. The other son, Edwin John (1895-
     ?), enlisted in the military in 1912. No other records were
     found for Edwin. Glen had a daughter, Patricia L. (Holland)
     Lowers, who died in 1996. She is also buried in Franklin Butte
     Cemetery in Scio, Oregon. http://www.rootsweb.ancestry.com/
     – orlinn/ see also Oregon State Archives and Patricia L. Lowers
     obituary, *Democrat-Herald*, Albany 12/2/1996.

251 Bates, op.cit.

252 Franklin Butte Cemetery records.

Epilogue
253 Smith, *Imperfect Pasture,* op.cit.

254 Righter, R.W. *Crucible for Conservation: The Struggle for Grand Teton National Park.* Colorado Associated University Press (1982), 192p.

BIBLIOGRAPHY

Books

Allen, M.V. *Early Jackson Hole*. Press Room Printing, Redding, CA (1981).

Andersen, J *The First Families into Jackson Hole*. Self published. Jackson Library Special Collection, Jackson, WY (1990).

Anderson, A.A. *Experiences and Impressions – The Autobiography of Colonel A.A. Anderson*. MacMillan Company, NY (1933).

Anderson, J. "Proving Up," in *Spindrift: Stories of Teton Basin*, Teton Arts Council, Driggs, Idaho (2000).

Baillie-Gorhman, W.A. *Camps in the Rockies*. Charles Scribner and Sons, New York (1882).

Bates, C. *Socio in the Forks of the Santiam*. Self Published. Socio, OR (1989).

Betts, R.B. *Along The Ramparts of the Tetons*. Assoc. University Press, Boulder, Co (1978).

Bonney, O.H. and L. Bonney. *Battledrums and Geysers: The Life and Journals of Lt. Gustaveous Cheney Doane*. Sage Books, Chicago (1970).

Bonney, O.H. and L.G. Bonney. *Bonney's Guide: Grand Teton National Park and Jackson's Hole*. Houston, TX (Trip 12, 1972).

Bradford, E. *Teton Jackson: The Life and Times of Jackson Hole's Famous Outlaw*. Mortimore Publishing, Lander, WY (2003).

Burt, S. *The Dairy of a Dude Wrangler*. Charles Scribner's Sons, NY (1924).

Calkins, F. *Jackson Hole*. Alfred A. Knopf, NY (1973).

Dary, D. *The Oregon Trail: An American Saga*. Knopf and Doubleday, NY. (2004).

Daugherty, J. et al. *A Place Called Jackson Hole*. National Park Service, Moose, WY (1999).

Diem, K., L. Diem, and W. Lawrence. *A Tale of Dough Gods, Bear Grease, Cantaloupe and Sucker Oil*. University of Wyoming-National Park Service Research Center, Moose, WY (1986).

Diem, K. and L. Diem. *A Community of Scalawags, Renegades, Discharged soldiers and Predestined Stinkers?* Grand Teton Natural History association, Moose, WY (1998).

Driggs, B.W. *The History of Teton Valley, Idaho*. Arnold Agency, Rexburg, Idaho (1970 ed.).

Dyke, J.C. *The West of the Texas Kid, 1881-1910; Recollections of Thomas E. Crawford*. University of Oklahoma Press, Norman (1962).

Hardee, J. *Pierre's Hole! The Fur trade History of Teton Valley, Idaho*. Sublette County Historical Society, Pinedale, WY (2010).

Harris, B. *John Colter, His Years in the Rockies*. (1993).

Huyler, J. *And That's the Way it Was in Jackson Hole*. Jackson Hole Historical Society and Museum, Jackson, WY (2003).

Jacoby, K. *Crimes Against nature: Squatters, Poachers, Thieves and the Hidden History of America.* University of California Press, CA (2001).

Johnstone, R.S., et al. *Inmates of the Idaho Penitentary* 1864-1947: A Comprehensive Catalog. Idaho State Historical Society, Boise (2008).

Kreps, B. *Windows to the Past: Early Settlers in Jackson Hole.* Jackson Hole Historical Society and Museum, Jackson, WY (2007).

Layser, E.F. "The Original natural Setting of Pierre's Hole: A Changed and Changing Landscape," in *Spindrift: Stories of Teton Basin.* Teton Arts Council, Driggs, Idaho (2000).

Layser, E.F. *I Always Did Like Horses and Women: Enoch Cal Carrington's Life Story.* Self published. Alta, WY (2008).

Layser, E.F. *Green Fire: Stories from the Wild.* Dancing Pine Publishing, Alta, WY (2010).

Madsen, B. *The Northern Shoshone.* Caxton Printers, Caldwell, ID (1980).

Mattes, M. *Colter's Hell and Jackson's Hole.* Chapter V. and *Jackson's Hole: Era of the Rocky Mountain Fur Company, VI.* in Les Trois Tetons: The Golden Age of Discovery. National Park Service, Moose, WY (1962).

Mumey, N. *The Teton Mountains: Their History and Tradition.* Aircraft Press, Denver (1947).

Nelson, F. *This Was Jackson Hole.* High Plains Press, Glendo, WY (1994).

Platts, D. *John Cherry: His Lies, Life and Legend.* Bearpaw Press, Jackson, WY (1991).

Platts, D. *The Cunningham Ranch Incident.* Self-Published. Wilson, WY (1992).

Platts, D. *Robert Miller: An Enigma.* Self-Published. Wilson, WY (2003).

Platts, D. *Teton Jackson Chief of Horsethieves.* Pine Hill Press, SD (2007).

Progressive Men of the State of Wyoming, A.W. Bowen & Company, (1901-1903 series).

Righter, R. *Crucible for Conservation: The Struggle for Grand Teton National Park.* Colorado Associated University Press (1982).

Righter, R. *A Teton Country Anthology.* Robert Reinhart, Inc. (1990). Robertson, M.E.W. (compiled by Judith Anderson).

Roosevelt, T. *The Wilderness Hunter: An Account of the Big Game of the United States and its Chase with Horse, Hound and Rifle* (1893). Republished by Sterling Publishers, Barnes and Noble Modern Edition (2012).

Ross, A. & K. Spaulding. *The Fur Hunters of the Far West.* University of Oklahoma Press, Norman (2001).

Russell, Osborne. *Journal of a Trapper.* University of Nebraska Press, NE (1955).

Sanborn, M. *The Grand Tetons: The Story of the Men Who Tamed the Western Wilderness.* G.P. Putnam's Sons, NY (1978).

Smith, B., E. Cole and D. Dobkin. 2004. *Imperfect Pasture.* U.S. Fish and Wildlife Service and Grand Teton Natural History association, Moose, WY (2004).

Sommers, J. *Green River Drift: A History of the Upper Green River Cattle Association*. Sky House Publishing, Helena, MT (1994).

Synder, G. *The Practice of the Wild*. Counterpoint, Berkley, CA (1900)

Talbot, V. *David E. Jackson: Field Captain of the Rocky Mountain Fur Trade*. Jackson Hole Historical Society and Museum, Jackson, WY (1996).

Thompson, E.M. and W.L. Thompson. *Beaver Dick: The Honor and the Heartbreak*. Jelm Mountain Press, Laramie, WY (1982).

Turiano, T. *Select Peaks of Greater Yellowstone*. Self published, Wilson, WY (2003).

Watson, J. *The Real Virginian: The Saga of Edwin Burham Trafton, Last of the Stagecoach Robbers*. Great West and Indian Series, V. 53, Western Lore Press, Tucson, Arizona (1989).

Wight, J. *The Jackson Hole Conspiracy*. Timbermill Press, Auburn, WY (2007).

Wilson, C.A. *The Return of the White Indian Boy*. (bound with *The White Indian Boy* by Elijah N. Wilson), University of Utah Press, Salt Lake City, Utah (1985).

Wister, O. *The Virginian*. MacMillian Co., NY (1902).

Wright, G. *People of the High Country: Jackson Hole before Settlers*. American University Studies, Vol. 7, NY (1984).

Periodicals, Journals, Collections, and Research Papers

Cannon, K.P. and M.B. Cannon, "Jackson Hole Bison Dig: Results of 2004 Field Investigations." National Park Service Midwest Archaeological Center, Lincoln, NE.

Crockett, S. "The Prehistoric Peoples of Jackson Hole," Chapter 2 in *A Place Called Jackson Hole*, pp 21-41, National Park Service, Moose, WY (1999).

Delacy, W.W. "A Trip Up the South Snake River in 1863," in Daugherty, J. et.al., *A Place Called Jackson Hole.* National Park Service, Moose, WY (1999).

DeLacy, W.W. "Contributions to the Historical Society of Montana 2," 1896.

Diem, K. and L. Diem Collection, Box 42, American Heritage Center, Laramie, WY.

Edith Thompson Papers, Undated Letter, Acc. 346, American Heritage Center, Laramie, WY.

"Gidden Letters," *Outdoor Life* (1902) in Allen, *Early Jackson Hole*, pp5-12.

Hill, C. et.al. "Caves of Wyoming." Geological Survey of Wyoming, University of Wyoming, Laramie, Bull. 59 (1976), pp347-351.

Hoyle, R.C. "To the Tetons by Train." CRM no. 10 (1999).

Irland, F. "The Wyoming Game Stronghold," *Scribner's Magazine*, Vol. 34: no. 3 (1903).

Moss, W. "Friend or Faux". *Teton Valley Top to Bottom Magazine.* Summer (2003), pp62-67

Owen, W. "Bill Barlow's Budget," June 9, 1892. Reprinted in the Jackson Hole Historical Society and Museum *Chronicle*, Fall 2006.

Roosevelt, T. "An Elk Hunt at Two Ocean Pass," *Century Illustrated Magazine*, Vol. XLIV, No. 6 (1892).

Stone, E.A. "Uinta County: Its Place in History" (1924). Jackson Hole Historical Society and Museum files, Jackson, WY (also on line).

USDA Forest Service Blackrock Ranger District Files: "Holmes' Cave History." Moran, WY.

Unpublished Memoirs

"Edith Thompson Papers," Acc. No. 346, American Heritage Center, Laramie, WY.

History of James H. Berger," compiled by Ron Berger and family, Troy, Idaho. 6p.

"Memoir of Mrs. Ervin Wilson (Mary Jane Lucus)" in Platts, *John Cherry (1853-1931): One of Jackson's Earliest Settlers.* Bearprint Press, Jackson, WY (1991).

"Memories of Charles W. Hedrick." Unpublished mimeo, November 1, 1948, 28p. (personal files of Harold Turner, Triangle X Ranch, Moran, WY).

Interviews and Personal Communication

Breckenridge, D. (grandson of David Breckenridge), pers. comm. with author, Tetonia, Idaho, 2012.

Carrington, E.C. Interview conducted by Clifford Hansen, University of Wyoming, 1957. American Heritage Center, Laramie, WY.

Croft, R. (granddaughter of Frank Petersen), pers. comm. with author, Lovell, WY, 2012.

Hansen, C. Interview with Pattie Layser, Jackson, WY, c2003 (published in *Teton Home* magazine, 2004).

Rudd, R. (local historian; friend of Slim Lawrence), pers. comm. with author, Victor, ID, 2012.

Turner, H. (Triangle-X Guest Ranch Partner, Guide and Outfitter), pers. comm..with author (2012).

National, State, and Local Archives

Bureau of Land Management, General Land Office Records and National Archives Homestead Case Files:
IDIDAA013924
IDIDAA048996 (Document 819)
IDIDAA048997 (Document 3074)
WYWYAA033418 (Document 91)
WYWYAA022417 (Document 35)
OROCAA043219 (Document 7028)
OROCAA047181 (Document 7514)

Affidavit of Witness for Enoch Carrington's Desert Entry in Teton

Basin, No. 3116, National Archives Case File.

U.S. 1900 Federal Census (Ancestry.com).

Teton County Courthouse Land and Water Records. Driggs, Idaho.

Teton County Courthouse Land and Patent Records, Driggs, Idaho.

Teton County Courthouse Land and Patent Records, Jackson, Wyoming.

Teton County, Idaho and Teton County, Wyoming Deed Books.

Franklin Butte, Oregon, Cemetery Records.

Newspapers

"It Happened long Ago." *Jackson Hole Courier*, May 20, 1954 (in Jackson Hole Historical Society and Museum "Settlers' File," Jackson, WY).

"Pioneer Civil War Vet Passes," July 16, 1931. No. 94, Box 2, Owen Collection, American Heritage Center, Laramie, WY(in the personal files of Loraine Bonney, Kelly, WY).

John Holland obituary: "Death of John Holland," *Santiam News,* June 1906.

Oregon Statesman, May 1906 and *Albany Democrat*, June 1906 (for details on the Socio, Oregon, fire).

Headlines on the massacre at Jackson Hole: *The New York Times*, *Baltimore Morning Herald*, and the *Cheyenne Tribune*, July 27, 1895.

Preparations for Jackson's Indian War defense and commentary: *Sun-Leader*, July-August 1895, Lander, WY.

Ed Harrington's Death: *Los Angeles Times*, 1922.

Other: See news articles contained in Wight, J. *The Jackson Hole Conspiracy* (2007).

World Wide Web (listed randomly)

http://www.ultimatewyoming.com (Union Pass Interpretation).

http://www.ancestry.com (U.S. Census records).

http:// Idaho State Historical Society reference Series Teton Jackson #451.

http://www.wyominggeneology.com/uinta/jacksons_hole_wyoming.htm (History of Uinta County and Teton Jackson).

http://www.wyomingtalesandtrails.com (Teton Jackson, Richard "Beaver-Dick" Leigh, et.al.).

http://www.rootsweb.ancestry.com/-wytetotp/bios1.htm (Bibliographies).

http://www.findagrave.com (John and Maud Holland).

http://www.glorecords.blm.gov/ (Homestead claims and records).

http://www.blm.gov/nhp/landfacts/ (Background and terminology).

http://rondiener.com/JHIW.htm (Diener, R.E., 2006, The Jackson Hole Indian War of 1895).

http://www.jsmacdonald@yellowstonemagic.com (History of Yellowstone Place Names).

http://www.nativeunity.blogspot.com/2007/09/beaver-dick-mountain man.com.

http://www.abish.byui.edu/specialcollections/manuscripts (Beaver Dick Leigh/ Forbush Interview by Vera Baldwin).

ABOUT THE AUTHOR

Earle F. Layser is a biologist, natural resources consultant, and author. He first came to Jackson Hole in 1947 with his parents. They camped out in the sagebrush in the back of a wood-paneled station wagon in full view of the Tetons. The author's career brought him back to Jackson Hole in 1976. Since then, over the years, he has maintained a special connection to the valley. His interests in Western history are reflected in the numerous history articles and books he has authored and published, including the award winning biography on Jackson Hole's colorful cowboy character, Enoch Cal Carrington: *I Always Did Like Horses and Women: Enoch Cal Carrington's Life Story*. In addition, he has also authored stories on a wide-variety of other subjects, including: farm and ranch, forestry, wildlife, natural history, and travel, which were published in a variety of magazines, journals, and anthologies. His 2010 book, *Green Fire: Stories from the Wild* has received local and regional acclaim as a conservation and natural history primer for the Northern Rockies and Greater Yellowstone region. The author resides in Alta, Wyoming, on the west-slope of the Tetons, with his wife Pattie, and their dog, Benji.

PRAISE FOR OTHER TITLES BY EARLE F. LAYSER

Green Fire: Stories from the Wild (2010)

The author has managed to blend science, myth, animal behavior and his own personal experience into a great contemporary natural history read. I learned things I didn't know about the creatures in my own back yard in Grand Teton National Park. I like this book a lot.
– Charlie S. Craighead, filmmaker, *Arctic Dance: The Murie Story* and author of *Who Ate the Backyard* and *Meet Me at the Wort*, Moose, Wyoming.

A champion of wildlife and nature, the author presents animals as heroes in his stories as they overcome challenges rooted in both nature and the encroachment of people into their habitat. Green Fire brings greater understanding and a desire for the protection and conservation of wildlife and the Earth's landscapes.
– Thomas D. Mangelsen, internationally acclaimed wildlife photographer and author of *Images of Nature and the Natural World*, Jackson, Wyoming.

Green Fire is a highly readable collection of wild animal stories ranging from the whimsical to the informed scientific. I would have to consult a dictionary to come up with enough good words to say about it. This book can serve as an ecological primer for the subject Rocky Mountain animals, their history and conservation, and their possible future prospects. I heartily recommend this book as a good read.
– Bert Raynes, naturalist and ornithologist, and weekly Jackson Hole News and Guide columnist, Director of the Meg and Bert Raynes Wildlife Fund, and author of *Valley So Sweet, Winter Wings, Birds of Grand Teton Park,* and *Birds of Sage and Scree*, Jackson, Wyoming.

I Always Did Like Horses and Women:
Enoch Cal Carrington's Life Story (2008)

*The author's thorough research and firsthand familiarity with the
Jackson Hole country breathes life into the odyssey of Cal Carrington.
Cal's fascinating story begins in Sweden, spans the continent of North
America and – by way of Teton Valley, Idaho, and Yellowstone –
ultimately provides keen insight into the lore of the Tetons. This book
deserves a spot in the library of any history buff – particularly those
interested in Jackson Hole.*
--Clifford P. Hansen, former U.S, Senator and Governor of Wyoming
and lifelong Jackson Hole rancher, Jackson, Wyoming.

*This biography is remarkable… It is the most highly documented
and extensively researched biography ever published of a notable
Jackson Hole character. It paints a realistic picture of the hard life of a
man as he struggles to make a place for himself in the Rocky Mountain
West. At the same time it provides abundant material on homesteading,
dude ranching, and the colorful inhabitants of early Jackson Hole and
Teton Valley.*
– Eugene Downer, publisher/editor *Teton Magazine*, Cloudcroft,
New Mexico.

A fascinating story … I enjoyed the book and admired the research.
– Lorraine Bonney, historian and coauthor of the ten *Bonney Guides*
for Wyoming, Kelly, Wyoming.

*Cal's story is marvelous … a fascinating look at a man, revealing a
complexity of character not appreciated in the legends about him. The
author really brings Cal and old-time Jackson to life … Should be on
every Western aficionado's bookshelf.*
--Jeanne Anderson, owner Dark Horse Bookstore, editor of *Spindrift:
Stories of Teton Basin*, Driggs, Idaho.

The author has done an admirable job of fleshing out Cal's story and establishing him in his own right as a truly colorful and historic figure. Cal moves between different cultures with remarkable ease and aplumb, but never loses his authentic Western character ... a welcome addition to the histories of the valley.
– Joe Arnold, artist and mountain climber, great-grandson of Eleanor "Cissy" Patterson, author of *Mountaineer's Dawn*, Laramie, Wyoming.

The author has diligently researched Cal Carrington's life ... what a great job! Wish I could have met Cal, he was a rare and authentic person ... a truly unique character of the Western past.
– Doris Platts, Jackson Hole historian, author of eight books on Jackson Hole and Western history, Wilson, Wyoming.